Jesus and Freedom

JESUS AND FREEDOM

Sebastian Kappen

ORBIS BOOKS

Maryknoll, New York

Library of Congress Cataloging in Publication Data

Kappen, Sebastian.
    Jesus and freedom.

    Bibliography: p.
    1.   Jesus Christ—Person and offices. 2.   Freedom
(Theology) 3.   Liberation theology. I.   Title.
PT202.K27   232   76-25927
ISBN 0-88344-232-9 Cloth
ISBN 0-88344-233-7 Paper

Contents

Preface

Though written down only in the course of the last year, the basic vision underlying *Jesus and Freedom* is the fruit of more than a decade of anguishing search for relevance, a search inspired largely by the many groups of students, seminarians, and intellectuals whom I had the privilege to address at seminars or in classrooms. It is they who made me ask questions that I had not dared to pose till then and embark on the arduous path of a radical criticism of the Christian faith. It is no less their positive and often enthusiastic response to my all too tentative interpretation of the message of Jesus that gave me the assurance that I am on the right track.

However, no claim is made that the views expressed here constitute my last word on the matter. Representing as it does a search that is not yet ended, the work contains quite a few statements that are exploratory regarding, if not content, at least formulation. Nevertheless I firmly believe that only an interpretation along the lines I have indicated does justice to the witness of the Gospels and to the requirements of our age.

The present work is addressed not to specialists but to the educated youth in India who may seek in the Gospels inspiration for radical commitment. The stress, therefore, is on projecting a vision rather than on providing a mass of information. In keeping with this aim I have tried to make the text as readable as possible. I have also avoided confronting the reader with the maze of the conflicting interpretations offered by biblical scholars. Instead I have put forward what seemed to me the best interpretation in each case without trying to justify them on exegetical grounds. Footnotes too have been reduced to the minimum. A select bibliography is given at the end as a help for further study.

I am deeply grateful to François Houtart, Director of the Centre for Socio-Religious Research, University of Louvain, Belgium, whose deep humanity and profound concern for the underprivileged all over the world have been a source of constant inspiration to me, for agreeing to write an introduction to my book. I should like to thank also M. S. Menon and Mary Samuel for going through the manuscript and suggesting improvements in style and presentation, and Josée Cleymans, who offered to type out copies for print.

The book will, I hope, be of help to the youth in other countries also who are grappling with the problem of the relevance of faith for the liberation of man.

Jesus and Freedom

Introduction

François Houtart

Sebastian Kappen's book is situated in a new stream of theology whose traces can be seen in different continents, more particularly in the theology of liberation that originated in Latin America, the black theology in South Africa, and also in the Philippines. A similar output is appearing in Europe and the United States at the present time, but, except for the black theology of the American Negroes, it is rather like an echo of what has been accomplished elsewhere. Even if European political theology has been able to inspire certain writers, particularly in Latin America, these same writers have rapidly achieved an independent production arising from the point of view they have adopted, which is the reference to the society in which this theological thought is produced.

The question that arises is to determine whether it is merely a fashion and a simple lag that is being progressively overcome, or a case of something quite different, and if so, of what? This is the question which this brief introduction would like to consider.

3

What Is a Theology?

A theology is a systematic reflection on a religious experience, an encounter between God and man (for the Christian, an encounter in Jesus Christ); the experience may be that of a religious founder, of prophets, of religious men, or of communities. These experiences are communicated in a certain language, in the form of a revealed or transmitted content, in symbolic expressions, or in ethical orientations. The gospel itself is already a transmission of the message and experience of Christ, through the religious experience of the Christian communities of that time.

Theology rests on these fundamental data and tries to elaborate a systematization between the various elements; to construct logic in function of the specific object that is proper to it; in short, to produce what is called a discourse on religion, or a 'meta-language'. The result is that theology does not develop in a void, but that it works on already existing material. It must, then, either explicitly or implicitly, define which material is valuable for systematic reflection and which can be admitted into the domain of religion or theology.

Moreover, the work of theology is not carried on in a methodological void. To systematize thought, use is made of philosophical references, formal logic, instruments of historical research; in short, theology draws a great number of its tools from the domains of culture and of knowledge. Indeed, this is one of the most fundamental reasons for the different theological approaches that have appeared throughout the course of time. The influence of Greek philosophy on St. Paul, for instance, or that of Aristotle on St. Thomas Aquinas, is well known. It is therefore very important to realize that theological thought is conditioned by the cultural environment and also to recognize the interrelationships existing between the culture and the other aspects of man's collective life, in its social, political, and economic organization.

Once expressed, a theological discourse acquires a certain autonomy, which is admittedly always relative, but which allows it to use this autonomy as one of the elements of subsequent reflection. This is a characteristic of all meta-language. Once uttered, it becomes a reality which must be taken into account and which can influence the course of events in different ways. A theological theory like that of predestination in Protestantism has had a great influence on certain cultural currents and even, as Max Weber has shown, on the evolution of various economic factors.[1]

However, two dangers threaten this type of language. The primary one is that of believing itself to be absolutely autonomous and hence forgetting the conditions of the starting point of its own work as well as of its contemporary production. In this case, theological thought risks being merely pure speculation detached from its foundations or risks unconsciously reflecting in an uncritical manner the ideas of its time, to which it has added a theological legitimation. And this is true in all the fields bordering on ethics, as well as those which are concerned with symbolic expressions, liturgical and even sacramental, just as much as for doctrinal elaboration. This is often easily perceived, as when, for instance, religious doctrines are explicitly used to justify a social order, but in other cases the mechanism is much more indirect and subtle and therefore difficult to perceive.

The second danger is that of becoming an institutional monopoly destined to control orthodoxy. Such a function, bound up with the responsibility of religious leaders, runs the risk of making theological work unproductive. In its constant reference to the original religious experience as well as to that of present-day persons and groups, this theological work should also exercise a critical function with respect to institutionalized religion.

All this is only the normal consequence of the process of the institutionalization of religion, as much in its existence as a more or less formalized group—and in the case of Catholicism, this factor is very important—as for theology itself. The important thing is to be conscious of this threat and to admit that theology is a work that is permanently in reference to a cultural, social, political, and economic environment, which is at one and the same time historical and contemporary. The creators of meta-language always tend to forget the very conditions of their scientific, artistic, cultural, or theological production and give too exclusive an importance to the autonomy of their work. On the contrary, acceptance of these influences is a condition of constant renewal in thought, for the reference to the real, that of the past re-read with new tools, or that of the present perceived in another way, is the source of the dynamism of all meta-languages, including theology.

Change of the Theological Locus

The locus forming the starting point of a theological reflection, that is, a reflection on the encounter between man and God, has undergone a rapid evolution. For a long time, it was centred on the religious group itself, as this was supposed to be the privileged place of the presence and of the action of God. Reference to "profane" society was mediated by that of the Church. That corresponded perfectly to the dominant situation in society of the religious group, or, after the destruction of the feudal system and the monarchy in Europe, to the possibility that existed for the Catholic Church to strengthen its system of thought and of organization, which it succeeded in doing so well that its autonomy lasted until Vatican II.

Today, it is precisely the locus of theological reflection that has changed. It has come to bear progressively more and more on man, and on man in society. This is the result of a long cultural and social transformation on which we shall not enter into in detail, but which had its roots in the birth of the mercantile capitalist system in Europe, in the Renaissance, and in the Reformation, each of these phenomena and many others having a dialectical relationship. Religion's function of furnishing the whole ideology of society progressively decreased and political thought, like all culture, eventually became centred on man. In the degree that theology did not take this emancipation of social and individual man as the locus for its reflection, in the same degree it implicitly accepted that this movement had become atheist.

The factor of knowledge plays an important role in this field; not because it enjoys complete autonomy in relation to other social realities, but because it influences the very perception of the religious dimension of human life. The absence of the knowledge of the mechanism by which collective life functioned in its economic, social, political, and cultural aspects, meant that the question of their causality was not asked, or if it was, that it was raised in immediately religious terms. Today, this is no longer possible. The question of the multiple causality of a social reality known to have been constructed is central. Social phenomena as results of human action are analyzed and recognized for what they are; this was not the state of knowledge in Palestinian society at the time of Jesus.

However, the phenomenon which we are now considering is even more precise. It is the question of the birth and evolution of a theology of liberation, in refer-

ence to a defined situation of alienation or dependence.
Now it is precisely in those regions of the world which
are regarded as 'peripheral' that this theology has appeared, in the countries that depend economically, politically, and culturally on the more or less marked dominance of the Western world. It is in these countries,
where social contradictions are the most apparent, that
theologians who, by profession and status do not belong
to the most oppressed classes, have perceived, analyzed,
and taken on themselves the condition of the oppressed.
No doubt, such an intellectual venture is not uncon-
nected with an on-going evolution in other parts of the
world and one can discern certain links with the political
theology and the theology of hope in Europe.[2] But the
latter have remained relatively timid and are still very
speculative. It is above all in Catholic Latin American
theology and in the Protestant South African theology
that the new orientations can be discerned.[3]

The attitude of these theologians is not the result of an
ethical reaction alone. Right throughout history, religious men have arisen vigorously against the abuse of
power and to denounce intolerable situations. An example that springs to mind is the Dominican theologian Las
Casas (1474–1566), who acted in support of the Indians in
Latin America. But what is new in the contemporary
movement is the utilization of a specifically analytical
intervention. The perception of social reality includes
not only the immediate misery and poverty, but the
mechanisms that are at the root of such situations. To the
admirable work of a Mother Teresa and of so many
others for the poorest of the poor must be added an
analysis that points to the fact that these poor are victims
of a social system and not simply of a natural fatality. The
development of the social sciences has allowed a progressively keener perception of these economic, social,

political, cultural, and psycho-social mechanisms. What characterizes the new theologies is the more or less explicit use of human sciences as tools to arrive at an understanding of social reality. However, if they are to be theologies, this knowledge must become a theological locus; in other words, the social situations to which reference is made must be considered as a place of encounter between God and man, a preferential place because of their determinative influence on all human life.

It can be said that this theological production is the result of the discovery of man, made long ago and influenced by the cultural changes in Europe at the end of the Middle Ages, and of the profound changes in the political, social, and economic systems that sustained them. More recently, 'social' man was discovered. This discovery was bound up with the development of an industrial and colonial capitalism which today has become monopolistic and international, and which has accentuated social contradictions.

At this stage of the reflection, a question can be asked about the influence of Marxism on such an approach. This question is important, for it is often raised by the opponents of the theology of liberation, who accuse it of being nothing more than a new version of Marxist thought and consequently of containing the virus of atheism. It is certainly true that the Marxian analysis of economic, social, and cultural conditions has greatly contributed to the knowledge of the mechanisms governing them. The work of the different schools of thought that refer to or are inspired by the analytical side of Marxism (historical materialism) have been at the basis of an important evolution in the social sciences, and there they have made a very important contribution. So it is clear that a theology that takes social reality as its theological locus cannot disregard the scientific contribution of Marxism. But it is also quite clear that there can be no question here of what Marx himself called a 'vulgar Marxism', reductionist, dogmatic, and simplistic, which is often put forward by its detractors, but also by certain of its adherents.

On the other hand, Marxism has inspired the major social and political movements of the present day in the line of a class struggle for economic, social, political, and cultural liberation. It is normal enough, then, that the inspiration for these movements be taken seriously by a theological reflection that is situated at the very core of their existence. If this were not done, it would result in an ideological appropriation that would not correspond to historical reality. But this does not mean that the theology of liberation renounces either its specificity or its critical function.

No doubt, philosophical materialism is not compatible with any theology, even a theology of liberation. But is it really necessary to associate the struggle for the liberation of the oppressed with atheism, and the justification for this oppression with religious faith? It is a question of practice more than of theory: when will religion cease being used as an instrument of domination, and when will the various religions, and particularly Christianity, stop allowing themselves to be used by the oppressor classes in the struggle they are conducting to maintain and increase their dominance? When shall we see a sufficient number of Christians committed to the struggle on the side of the oppressed so that the credibility of their action will have not only a personal but a collective witness?

When we speak of a question of practice, this means something beyond discourse and even beyond theology. An authentic theology of liberation, moreover, cannot be separated from social practice and it is because of this that certain people have said, and correctly if the real meaning of the expression is grasped, that orthopraxy precedes orthodoxy. Kappen has understood this well and this is why his approach stems from the heart of Indian reality, which is the locus of his reflection, even if this is later enlarged by a retro-reflection on the experience and message of Jesus.

It is inevitable that the theology of liberation provokes reactions. The more immediate arise in theological trends which feel that their very methodological foundations are put into question. Sometimes the opposition is based on an ideological argument: a theology that takes sides can no longer be a credible discipline. A theologian such as G. Girardi has answered this by saying that a 'theology of omission' is also ideologically conditioned, but without being aware of it and this prevents it from being critical of its presuppositions. This kind of discussion takes place around other levels of the meta-languages, around the social sciences, and even in the exact sciences, although for reasons that are epistemologically rather different.

But there are even more subtle ways of blocking the proposed approach. One of them consists in using the same vocabulary, but giving it a different meaning. Liberation acquires an exclusively spiritual sense: Christian liberation is liberation from sin, and a scriptural basis is not wanting to justify this affirmation. This point of view cannot be denied, but when it becomes a matter of contention, 'liberation' takes on another meaning and becomes the negation of the perception of social contradictions as a locus of Christian awareness and action. Finally, another method that is quite common today is to use the concepts of the theology of liberation in ecclesiastical documents and even in the acts of the magisterium, but without this usage having any consequences on the

institutional practice of the Church, either in its relationships with society or in its internal organization.

In certain countries, those who produce this theology
have met with civil repression, for in societies where the
symbolic power of religion is great, a theological criticism
of society can be socially efficacious. The secular power
relies on the perhaps tacit support of religious groups.
The liberal mentality of the new capitalist elites of the
majority of the countries of Asia, Latin America, and
Africa lying within the Western orbit, can adapt itself to
verbal criticism, but only when there is no risk of its
becoming effective in the field of social relationships. As
soon as the least danger arises, measures are taken,
sometimes with the connivance of the religious authorities. This type of behaviour shows, *a contrario*, the
validity of the approach of the theology of liberation.

But when all is said and done, the question arises as to
whether the methodological approach is not essentially
Western, and to what degree Eastern thought can make
its contribution.[4] This is an objection that has been
raised. The author of this Introduction is certainly not
competent to answer this objection, but can put forward
a few reflections on this subject. First, it is a fact that the
capitalist economic system is dominant in all nonsocialist
Asian societies. That is to say that it exercises an incon-
testable domination over the traditional sectors of the
socio-economic organization and of the ideology: only
insofar as they are useful to the dominant sector are the
others allowed to exist or to develop as dependent forms.
The objective basis of a class society is thus established,
even if other forms still exist as determinants of social
relationships (e.g., castes), or even if the class consciousness is not yet shared by all the strata of the population. Moreover, the dominant class, even if it styles
itself socialist out of political necessity, shares the liberal

ideology which is typical of bourgeois elites throughout the world, and diffuses a conception of development which allows it effectively to absorb the surplus that is produced at the base: work and discipline are the key factors in development, but mention is rarely made of the social structure (the social relationships of production) which effects an unequal distribution of the fruits of labour.

In Asia, also, there are political movements inspired by Marxism which are playing an important role in the reorganization of Asian societies. To speak of one case only, the Democratic Republic of North Vietnam has succeeded, in spite of the war, in remodelling a society that was in bad shape after the colonial experience, and in organizing it on a new basis, where food, work, and health are recognized and assured as the essential rights of every human person. However, one cannot say that Vietnam has lost its own culture and its own modes of thought. The contrary is true. The real grass-roots participation in the organization of production and in the distribution of the fruits of labour, has created a new zone of liberty which was previously unknown to the greater part of the population. Marxism, which is of Western origin, has been used as a social and ideological tool, but Eastern thought has not been excluded because of that. Whatever may be the situation elsewhere, or whatever one may think of it, the existence of countries organized on this model and the existence of political currents and popular movements inspired by Marxism are undeniable facts.

The very difficult problem of the relationship between culture and the socio-economic organization can only be referred to here. There can be no doubt that Eastern thought cannot remain unaltered when faced with the transformation of social realities, any more than Western thought did. But the very condition of its dynamism is to accept the on-going dialectical process, and the fact that an Asian theology of liberation can be conceived of already opens up an important field of work for the future.

The Originality of the Approach

Kappen believes in the force of the gospel as practice and as project and, with many others, he is struck by the contradiction existing between liberation and religion, and particularly the message of Christ in its institutional reality. At the beginning, he reveals the locus from which he speaks and for that he outlines an analysis of it. He is speaking from India and does not produce theology for the planet Mars. Many may wonder why he begins with chapters that have no theological content. We have given the reason for this above. It is a question of a new approach, bound to the social experience of the group of which the author is speaking and to which he himself belongs. This collective experience is perceived with new tools of analysis today. This is the role of the human sciences.

But one can choose from several types of analysis, and how to make one's choice? In certain works, Indian society is shown in its industrial and cultural dynamism with the progress accomplished since independence translated into statistics of production, educational institutions, or formation of intellectuals; this progress is undeniable. However, it is an analysis made from the top of the social ladder. What does one see if one looks from lower down? Another analysis has to be made, in another theoretical framework and using other means of observation or other gauges. It is the latter that Kappen has chosen. It could be said that this choice is ideological. Obviously yes, quite simply because he believes that fidelity to Christ demands an option in favour of the poor and the oppressed. Sensitivity and openness to their point of view is required. This point of departure, which in no way invalidates the analytical approach itself but which serves rather to locate it clearly, is opposed to that which is most often conveyed in Christian circles that are strongly influenced by a liberal bourgeois ideology, by an elitist vision of society, and by the view of development which we have described earlier.

After developing this perspective, the author returns to Jesus, to his experience and his teaching. He does this, not in the hope of finding there direct answers to all the present-day problems of Indian society, nor to justify his ideological or political options by means of isolated texts, but as a global questioning of the present-day social practice of a disciple of Christ. Fundamentally, it is a matter of re-reading the Gospels in the light of the challenge raised by today's oppressed. But Kappen goes further in his methodological approach. He uses the instruments of recent knowledge (social theories and analysis) to approach the gospel reality. He is one of the first to approach the problem in this fashion and his creativity is shown most strikingly here. Others have worked at this task, but Kappen has done it with the sensibility of an Eastern man and of one who is, moreover, in constant contact with the suffering reality of Indian society.[5]

Another very important perspective which is developed in this work is that of placing Jesus in the prescientific culture of his time. Probably the author has been helped in this approach by his contact with the ordinary masses sharing this type of culture, with the richness that it entails in the apprehension of all reality as a global entity, of a noncompartmentalized life, but which also entails some difficulty in gaining access to a knowledge of causality. It is in this framework that he treats of the miracles, as an expression of the mission of Christ and of his victory over evil and oppression, which must be interpreted today as political tasks.[6]

The present current of the theology of liberation scarcely allows for individual and personal aspects of the expression of faith, which is understandable, seeing its object. However, Kappen approaches the subject and integrates it into his general vision. This is another new contribution which offers a basis for a complete theological vision. For all these reasons, this work is, at one and the same time, an important contribution to thought and a witness which all those who want to work on the side of the oppressed, in reference to Jesus Christ, will welcome with deep joy.

NOTES

1. Max Weber, *The Protestant Ethic and the Spirit of Capitalism*, trans. Talcott Parsons (New York: Scribner's, and London: Allen and Unwin, 1956).

2. J. B. Metz, *Theology and the World*, trans. William Glen-Doepel (New York: Herder, 1969).

3. Gustavo Gutiérrez, *A Theology of Liberation*, trans. Sister Caridad Inda and John Eagleson (Maryknoll, N.Y.: Orbis Books, 1973); B. Moore, *Black Theology—the South African Voice* (London: Hurst and Co., 1973).

4. Raimundo Panikkar, "Philosophy and Revolution: The Text, the Context, and the Texture," *Philosophy East and West* 23 (July 1973) 315–22.

5. F. Belo, *Lecture matérialiste de l'Evangile de Marc* (Paris: Le Cerf, 1974); José Miranda, *Marx and the Bible: A Critique of the Philosophy of Oppression*, trans. John Eagleson (Maryknoll, N.Y.: Orbis Books, 1974).

6. Jürgen Moltmann, *The Gospel of Liberation*, trans. H. Wayne Pipkin (Waco, Texas: Word Books, 1973).

I

The Quest and the Questions

Our age is marked by a heightened awareness of the many forces that oppress man and prevent his spontaneous unfolding into rich and meaningful existence. Many find in religion itself a force for oppression, and are convinced that the sooner it disappears, the better for the future of mankind. Others, while granting that many historical forms of religion have played, and are still playing, a reactionary role by legitimizing and reinforcing systems of unfreedom, believe that authentic religiosity can be a potential for liberation. It is this latter conviction that impelled us to conduct an investigation into the relevance of Jesus for the integral liberation of man.

Every investigation proceeds from its own assumptions, which determine its general approach and method. Our basic assumptions are twofold: that it is necessary to go back to the original message of Jesus, and that it is equally necessary to reinterpret it in the context of the self-understanding of contemporary man. The validity of these assumptions will, we hope, become clear in the course of the investigation itself. In this chapter we do no more than make a few preliminary remarks to help the reader to participate better in our search.

It is necessary to go back to the historical Jesus because his original message is much more relevant for us than

17

most subsequent interpretations, which have either rendered it innocuous or even distorted it. To grasp this it is necessary to dwell on the history of Christian alienation.

Jesus Alienated

The alienation of Christian faith and practice from the historical Jesus took place along three principal lines —cultic, dogmatic, and institutional. For an adequate grasp of this process it would be necessary to go back to the very sources of Christianity and from there to trace its development right up to our own day. This is not possible within the limited scope of this book. What is attempted here is nothing more than a schematic and, admittedly, simplified outline of the more salient features that stand out even on cursory analysis.

Cultic alienation was the first to set in. The historical Jesus devalued cult by subordinating it to justice, mercy, and love. He did not project himself as an object of worship. He did not institute any rite that can be called cultic in the traditional sense of the term. But no sooner did he die than there developed a cult centered upon him. However, its focal point was not the Jesus of history but the Jesus risen from the dead and seated at the right hand of the Father. The Jesus who was a part of our history was replaced in Christian piety by the risen Christ, regarded as above history, as eternal and immutable. The same piety removed him from our midst, from the common run of everyday life, and installed him in the tabernacle. It built a separate home for him furnished with flowers, candles, holy water, and incense. It projected him as a stickler for ritual purity, who avoided publicans and sinners and looked down upon the 'pro-

---

The substance of this chapter appeared in the form of an article under the title "Jesus Today" in *Jeevadhara* 27, Theology Centre, Alleppey (May–June 1975) 169–81.

fane' world of everyday life. Cult also started a process of abstraction. The death of Jesus was dissociated from his historical life or reduced to a mere prerequisite for resurrection. Jesus was further fragmented into many formal aspects, each of which in its turn became the object of a new 'devotion'. Thus we had a plethora of devotions having for their objects the 'Precious Blood', the 'Crown of Thorns', the 'Five Wounds', the 'Sacred Heart'. By the Middle Ages Christianity had become a cult-centred religion. Mercy, justice, and love became secondary to the Eucharistic cult and the devotions. The circle was complete. A noncultic prophetic movement had ended up as a cultic religion.

The history of dogma and catechesis shows a parallel process of alienation. Jesus as pictured in the Synoptic Gospels is a man among men, a member of the family of man. He was less word made flesh than flesh become word, matter endowed with a tongue. Flesh of our flesh, blood of our blood, he learned to love by being loved by others, gained knowledge of himself in being acknowledged by others. It was in meeting his kind that he learned kindness and compassion. He loved man. He struck root in others to such an extent that they became a need for him especially in moments of crisis. Exquisitely attuned to everything human, he valued the friendship of women; loved children, wine, and the lilies of the field. He could rejoice with those who rejoiced and weep with those who wept.

Like any man he too had to grow in wisdom and in favour with God and man (Luke 2:52). He was a quester after truth, after the God who made him. And he found him on the banks of the Jordan River. On the day of his baptism at the hands of John the Baptizer he was taken hold of by God. He was swept off his feet, uprooted from his familiar world, and transplanted into the realm of the divine. There he was given a new mind and a new heart, and he began to see the world in a new light, in the light of the reign of God. But his search did not end there. He had still to come to terms with God and reach a point of clarity regarding his mission in life. The consequent inner struggle with light and darkness is represented in the Gospels as the temptations in the desert.

Jesus was also fully conscious of his limitations. Asked about the final coming of the Kingdom, he replied, "But about that day or that hour no one knows, not even the angels in heaven, not even the Son, only the Father" (Mark 13:32). So too he admitted openly that he could not dispense the blessings of the age to come just as he liked. The sons of Zebedee who sought the favour of being allowed to sit in state one on his right, the other on his left, were told bluntly that to sit at his right or left was not for him to grant, that it was for those to whom it had already been assigned (Mark 10:40). Though the divine was in him radiating his power, he did not think to snatch at equality with God (Phil. 2:6). When a stranger called him 'good master' his answer was: "Why do you call me good? No one is good except God alone" (Mark 10:17–18).

Like any other man he was subject to varying and conflicting emotions. The woes he uttered against the hypocrites of his day betray a spirit that was quick to flame with indignation. He was filled with anger at the sight of the trafficking that went on in the temple, the house of his Father. The destiny he was to meet in Jerusalem set every fibre of his being in tension. "I have a baptism to undergo, and what constraint I am under until the ordeal is over" (Luke 12:50). The prospect of death was to him a source of infinite sadness which he wanted to share with his friends: "My heart is ready to break with grief" (Mark 14:34). It filled him with fear and anguish. To quote the writer of the Letter to the Hebrews: "In the days of his earthly life, he offered up prayers and petitions, with loud cries and tears, to God who was able to deliver him from the grave" (Heb. 5:7).

What a far cry from this Jesus, who is so much like us and yet in his very likeness stands out as the wholly other, is the Christ of dogma! The latter is Jesus transmuted as he was made to pass through the Greco-Roman mould of thinking. He came out of this mould fragmented into abstractions such as person, nature, hypostasis, body, soul, substance, quality, quantity, essence, and existence. What cult did at the level of action, theology did at the level of thought. Jesus was reduced to a mere sum of formal concepts. Seen from the human plane he is a man with two natures subsisting in one divine person; seen from the divine plane he is the second person of the Trinity, identical in nature with the Father and the Holy Spirit. Controversies raged as to whether the Spirit proceeds from the Father only or from the Father and the Son. What is worse, in this process of sterile philosophical reflection the humanity of Jesus was downgraded. Of course dogma as well as theology affirmed his human nature but not without denying him the status of a human person, a mode of reasoning that sounds very odd to us. This had its repercussion in popular catechesis. For the mass of believers Jesus appeared as God under the guise of man. In their eyes he did not really grow in wisdom; for, being God, he knew from early infancy all there is to know. Though they recited the official creed, which said that he suffered under Pontius Pilate, they knew well enough that he could not have *really* suffered, endowed as he was on earth with the beatifying vision of God. If ever they read the Gospels, they slurred over the passages that affirmed his human condition or, if clever enough, managed to put dishonest interpretations on them. In short, if cult segregated him from the company of man and settled him down in churches on the fringes of the real world, dogma banished him to the world of ideas. In this process the Jesus of history became a forgotten person.

No less than cult and catechesis did institutionalism distort the image and the teachings of Jesus. The Gospels picture him as one who right from the outset of his public life rejected power, whether economic or political, as a means to usher in the New Age. And the historical movement he set in motion was one predominantly of the poorer classes in Palestine and the Greco-Roman world who had no political ambitions. But with Emperor Constantine, who declared Christianity the state religion, the leaders of the Christian community began to enjoy economic and political privileges. The temptation Jesus overcame in the desert his disciples succumbed to all too easily. The Church began to exercise control over every sphere of life. This led to a proliferation of institutions. Though in course of time political life regained its autonomy vis-à-vis the Church, the latter held on to its institutions—schools, colleges, hospitals, and orphanages—and even started new ones. Every local church has today its institutional empire. What is still more saddening is that most of these institutions have not even an umbilical bond with the gospel of Jesus. By and large they embody the values of capitalism—private interest, competition, aggression, and lust for power. Besides, insofar as they violate the legitimate autonomy of secular spheres of life, they have become even instruments of domination. Thus by a curious development the good news of liberation preached by Jesus gave rise to structures of unfreedom. Institutionalism has in this manner disfigured his image and neutralized the revolutionary, disruptive force of his teaching.

The tragic consequence of all this is that Jesus of Nazareth is the most forgotten person among the very

people who claim to be his disciples. He lies buried
under the weight of accumulated layers of rituals, rubrics, laws, concepts, legends, myths, superstitions, and
institutions. He lies bound hand and foot by innumerable cords that tradition has cast around him. His voice is
smothered, his spirit stifled. If he still acts and makes his
presence felt in history, it is less through the official
Church than through honest dissenters among Christians. Therefore it is the duty of all who cherish the vision
and hope of Jesus to set him free from the prison-house
of cult, dogma, and institutionalism so that he can freely
go about pointing, as of old, his accusing finger at the
scribes, pharisees, elders, priests, and Herods of today.
To this end it is necessary to remove the many veils that
historically conditioned faith and tradition have put on
him, and let his visage shine forth in its original splendour, and his words ring out in their untamed incisive-
ness.

What we have said thus far should not be interpreted
to mean that the history of Christianity until now has
only been one of progressive alienation. The development of Christian theory and practice in the West contains also positive elements in harmony with the teachings of Jesus. These elements have to be clearly distinguished from those that are at variance with it. Such a
critical study may be useful, and even necessary, up to a
point, but should never be made an absolute for people
who do not share the Western tradition. If we Indians
have no other way to meet God as revealed in the life and
teachings of Jesus than by mentally reenacting the history of Western Christianity we are of all men the most to
be pitied.

We have seen that it is necessary to go back to the
historical Jesus. But is not the attempt doomed to fail
considering that the Gospels are not historical docu-

ments in the usual sense of the term but the expression of the faith of the early Christians? This is a serious problem on which an adequate discussion, though useful, is not possible within the scope of this chapter. This much, however, may be said. It is true that the nature of our sources renders futile any attempt to write a biography or psychology of Jesus. It is impossible to reconstruct the sequence of events in his life. But to go further and say that no understanding of the historical Jesus at all is possible is unwarranted. The Gospels are the concrete embodiment of the response of the early Christians to an *historical* reality: to the life, words, and deeds of Jesus of Nazareth. Hence it is possible for us to have a real encounter with the historical Jesus in and through the Gospels. Using the criteria provided by contemporary biblical criticism we can arrive at an adequate grasp of the person and teachings of Jesus, which are themselves events in history, and perhaps also, of a very broad outline of his life.[1] Nothing more is presupposed in this book.

However, this is no plea for rediscovering the historical Jesus in order to mimic him or to repeat parrotwise his teachings. His message needs to be reinterpreted in a spirit of creative fidelity.

Jesus Beyond Jesus

The need for such a reinterpretation was precluded by the traditional approach, which all too one-sidedly emphasized the divinity of Jesus to the neglect of his humanity. To those who saw him primarily, if not exclusively, from the plane of the divine it was but natural to conclude that his teaching in all its details was eternally and immutably true.

But this whole approach is to be called in question. It was not from above nor from the angle of preconceived notions that his contemporaries saw him. They saw him from below as a man among men, as the carpenter from Nazareth. It was in observing his ordinary human behaviour—his words, gestures, and actions—that they gained a glimpse into the divine dimension in him. Their approach should be normative for us too. The recognition of Jesus as a member of the human family must be the point of departure of all our reflections. But to recognize him as man is to regard him as rooted in the soil, as inserted in the current of history. And as part of history, he shared the mode of thinking that prevailed among his people.

Now, the ideas and beliefs of any people bear the imprint of their social system constituted by the mode of production, the stratification of classes, and the structure of political power. Any significant change in the social base implies also a corresponding change in the system of ideas and beliefs. The self-understanding of man in a tribal society is not the same as that of man in feudal society, or that of a member of the capitalist society. It is therefore evident that Jesus, who lived twenty centuries ago, viewed nature, man, and God differently from us.

This does not mean that his teachings contain nothing of perennial value. Even people of earlier ages could have gained profound insights valid for all times, though cast in outmoded conceptual moulds. This is all the more true of prophetic individuals who emerge in periods of cultural crisis. They give articulate expression to the revolt against the past and the longing for the new, which exist in an inarticulate, confused manner among the masses. They are essentially heralds of the future, men who dream new dreams and see new visions. Their destiny is to leap into the unknown ahead and carry the masses with them. They are gripped by the ultimate concern of life and, therefore, their message necessarily has something of the unconditioned. Both in their revolt against the status quo and in their commitment to the not-yet there is much that is valid for men of all times. Yet in the very breakthrough they achieve at the level of the total vision of man, they remain conditioned by the status quo they revolt against. The new they can envisage only in the language of the old. Even the very content of their message exhibits this tension between the not-yet and the already, between the absolute and the relative. Though lonely in the sweep of their vision and the passion of their commitment, they still remain very much men of their age.

Jesus of Nazareth was one such prophet—so transcendent in his vision, yet so immanent in his world; so perennial in his appeal, yet so rooted in his age; so absolute in his demands, yet so conditioned by his environment. His message comes to us cast in a cultural mould we have long left behind. Hence the need to reinterpret it in the light of our contemporary experience by distinguishing its perennially valid elements from the historically conditioned, and by bringing to light its deeper implications for the man of today.

But, in trying to reinterpret Jesus for the contemporary world, are we not committing the same mistake as did the early and subsequent generations of Christians? Are we not distorting his image to suit our tastes and safeguard our interests? That there is such a danger cannot be denied. And the only way to avoid it is to see to it that our interpretation is not naive but critical. But what are the criteria that should guide such criticism? They are twofold: fidelity to the original Jesus-phenomenon and responsiveness to the God who reveals himself to us in history.

Christians of the first centuries could not have applied the first criterion. For they lived in an age in which the boundary between myth and reality was blurred. Reality tended to be mythicized; and myth, to be looked upon as history. Consequently, it was natural for the early Christians to raise Jesus to the status of a mythical person. Criticism in our sense of the term was therefore not possible for them. Quite different is our situation. We have gone beyond the stage of primitive myth. We know that any valid interpretation has to be in the nature of a response to historical phenomena as we encounter them. This obliges us at every stage to subject our subjective prejudices and preferences to criticism lest they colour our interpretation of reality.

Let us now come to the second criterion. In the message of Jesus there is an absolute and a relative dimension. The absolute dimension can be explained only on the basis of his encounter with the Absolute, with God. But precisely because this encounter was enfleshed in a historical situation, it is possible and even natural that the total significance of it overflowed the limits of what was explicitly perceived by Jesus himself. This is in fact true of all aesthetic and religious encounters with truth. That is why the truth of a work of art is often perceived more fully by the viewer than by the artist himself. Similarly, it is only subsequent generations that understand the total meaning of a great thinker or religious genius. However, any subsequent interpretation has to be in line with the fundamental thrust and implicit dynamism of the original datum. Now the fundamental dynamism of Jesus' message pointed to God working in history. If our reinterpretation of Jesus is to be authentic, it is essential that we encounter in history the same God whom he encountered two thousand years ago. It is our responsiveness to the God of today that guarantees our fidelity to the Jesus of yesterday. The demands that God in history makes on us help us understand the deeper meaning of the teachings of Jesus. Conversely, the teachings of Jesus help us interpret the signs of the times and decipher the divine challenges inscribed in history. In this way the Jesus of history enters into dialogue, in and through us, with the God of today.

However, the encounter with God in question is not to be understood solely in a mystical or esoteric sense. Any man gripped by an absolute concern for his fellowmen has encountered God. It is possible, even likely, that the extreme radicals who are in prison today for the sole crime of having opposed an unjust society had a more authentic encounter with God than many professedly religious men and women who devote themselves to prayer and penance. For the same reason the former may understand the significance of Jesus much better than the latter.

If, therefore, we retrace our steps back to Jesus of Nazareth it is not to pitch our tent with him but to go beyond him. We go beyond him when we free his message from its historical conditioning and translate it into today's language. In other words, we make it possible for him to go beyond himself and discover his true identity in our age. We let him slough off the past in order to come alive in the present, but not without carrying with him whatever in his past has an abiding value. Thus we raise him from the dead and give him a new name and habitation. Seen in this light, the resurrection of Jesus is a continuing process achieved through our reinterpretation of his message and our commitment in response to it.

A reinterpretation of the entire message of Jesus along these lines is an urgent need of our time. This, however, is beyond the scope of our investigation. We confine ourselves to just one question: What is the relevance of the message of Jesus for human liberation today? In seeking an answer our primary source is the Synoptic Gospels. Though they too are expressions of the faith of the early Christian community, in their case, as contrasted with the fourth Gospel, the veil of interpretation is not so thick as to prevent our gaining an insight into the salient features of the life and teachings of the historical Jesus.

The self-revelation of God in history is the light in which we have to reinterpret the message of Jesus, and, as such, should be the point of departure of all theological reflection. We shall therefore begin with an analysis of the Indian situation in order to focus the challenge of liberation it poses. The subsequent chapters will deal with the response, in word and deed, of Jesus to the varied forms of human bondage. In the concluding chapter we shall derive from our study some fundamental guidelines for action.

NOTE

1. On this question, see Günther Bornkamm, *Jesus of Nazareth* (London: Hodder and Stoughton, 1960; New York: Harper, 1961), pp. 13–27; Norman Perrin, *Rediscovering the Teaching of Jesus* (London: SCM, and New York: Harper, 1967), pp. 207–48; James M. Robinson, *A New Quest of the Historical Jesus*, Studies in Biblical Theology, 25 (London: SCM, and Naperville, Ill: Allenson, 1959).

II

The Challenge of Liberation

The forces of oppression in contemporary India are many and varied. Some have their roots in feudalism, which in one form or another still persists, especially in rural areas; others stem from capitalism which, though originally imposed from outside, has become deeply entrenched in the soil and today controls the entire economy. Some are found at the level of the economic, social, and political life of the people; others at the level of beliefs, ideas, and values. Some exist as objective factors that are relatively autonomous in relation to individual options; others are lodged in the subjectivity of man as a personal and unique centre of decision. In what follows we shall try to describe briefly the basic structures and forces of oppression in our country.

Slavery Reborn

By far the majority of the Indian population are workers employed either in agriculture or industry. Landless labourers alone make up roughly 40 percent of the rural population. Many among the small peasants including tenants and sharecroppers, who form 45 percent of the rural population, are forced by economic necessity either to sell their land and join the ranks of landless labourers or to take to wage labour as an additional source of income. Urban workers of all types and their families amount to roughly 40 million.[1] The working classes, to whichever category they belong, are the real creators of wealth and form the backbone of the country. And yet, work for them is a process in which they fashion their own fetters and strengthen the hands of their oppressors. To realize what this means we must reflect on the existing system of production.

Work, where it is truly human, is a process of the humanization of nature, of the environment. Workers take the stuff of the earth into their hands, breathe their spirit into it, and fashion it in their own image. Thereby they give it a new form, unity, and meaning—all drawn from the wealth of their own being. The products of labour are therefore the embodiment of their spirit, the extension of their being in time and space. Seen in this light, the civilization that is being constructed around us is nothing but the physical and mental energies of the working class, dead and buried in matter and risen again in the form of things useful and beautiful. If this is true, the conclusion imposes itself that the products of work must belong to the producers.

But the opposite is what happens in the present economic system. The products are expropriated from the producers. It is not those who till the soil who eat the fruits of the soil. It is not those who make cars that travel in them. It is not those who produce costly foods that consume them. Those who make sophisticated garments go about clad in rags. Those who build mansions are condemned to live in slums. Those who build luxury hotels and posh restaurants are unable to afford even one full meal a day. Those who produce antibiotics and costly drugs are denied even the minimum of medical care when they themselves fall ill. In short those who create wealth are reduced to utter poverty. They are denied not only luxuries and utilities but also the bare necessities of life. All this is a matter of common observation. It is also borne out by the studies of experts in the field. According to one such study, 40 percent of the rural poor and 50 percent of the urban poor live below the poverty line both in terms of calories and of quality of nutrition, as of 1960. The increase since then in consumer expenditure (one-half of one percent per annum) has benefitted mainly the rich. During the past decade, while the condition of the rural poor has remained stagnant, that of the urban poor has deteriorated.[2]

It follows from what we have said so far that the most intensely felt bondage of the Indian masses consists in the fact that they do not have what they produce. They do not have what they produce because they are deprived of the means of production, agricultural as well as industrial. Land, the means of agricultural production, is concentrated in the hands of the big peasants and landlords, either because land reform laws are inadequate or have been poorly implemented. Taking operational holdings in the country as a whole, roughly 36 percent of the rural households either did not cultivate any land or cultivated only less than half an acre each; 57.9 percent of rural households cultivate either no land or less than 2.5 acres each. They operate no more than 7 percent of the total land. On the other hand, we have a privileged 2.09 percent of households that cultivate more than 30 acres each, which, when added, comes to 23 percent of the total land.[3]

No less glaring is the concentration of the means of industrial production. The big bourgeoisie consisting of about 75 to 100 business houses own 50 percent of all private company assets in India.[4] The policies pursued by the Government in respect of licensing and financial and technical assistance have themselves contributed to the concentration of wealth and income in restricted groups.[5] Even the so-called public sector has worked to the benefit of the private sector. Contrary to popular belief, the interests of private business do not usually come into conflict with those of the public sector, which consists mainly of big industries where private investment is not forthcoming. The public sector in fact feeds the private sector by providing it at cheap price with the goods it needs, by entrusting to it much of its own construction works, and by buying up its products.[6]

That the mass of producers are deprived of both the means and the fruits of production is the aspect of economic bondage that is most acutely felt. But, objectively, the most dehumanizing aspect is less the expropriation of products than the depersonalization of the producers. For the worth of a man is to be judged less in terms of what he *has* than in terms of what he in reality *is*. Consumerism has so shaped our thinking that even when we criticize capitalism we often do so with criteria derived from the same system. All the greater, therefore, is the need to highlight the existential degradation of the working class in contemporary Indian society.

Man is *essentially* a worker. In a sense he *is* his work. Work is not something added on to his essence already complete and rounded off in itself. His essence is what he makes of himself in the process of work. If so, to be deprived of work is to be denied the possibility of being human, of realizing what he ought to be. It is in this light that we have to view the problem of unemployment, which is steadily increasing. According to one estimate, one out of every ten Indians is unemployed.[7] Still more staggering is the problem of underemployment. Forty per cent of the rural population live below the national desired minimum of a per-capita income of Rs. 240 per annum as of 1961 prices. Leaving out another ten percent whose lot can be improved only through social services, we still have 30 percent of the rural poor numbering roughly 128.5 million who are poor because they are underemployed.[8] This means that millions of our brothers and sisters are denied even the minimum of participation in economic life and have been brutally marginalized.

In the case of those partially or fully employed there is no freedom in the choice of work. The choice of work is subject to the law of supply and demand in the labour market. People are forced to take up jobs for which they are not suited, just because they have no other way to make a living. For them work is not an expression of a spontaneous urge. The same unfreedom is experienced also in the place of work, whether it is field or factory. There they engage in the production of goods which they themselves cannot afford. They work for goals in the choice of which they have no say, and for the satisfaction of other people's needs. Once they enter the place of work they belong not to themselves but to their employers, who dispose of them as they would things. Barred from employing their intelligence and initiative in determining goals and choosing means, they are reduced to the position of mere cogs in the wheel, of so many units of muscular energy expended to make machines run. They are like things that can safely be thrown away once they have served their purpose. What is worse, in producing goods they are in truth fashioning their own shackles, providing their masters with ever-new instruments of exploitation. Wage labour of this type is slavery reborn in a new form. It is a process whereby the masses in humanizing nature dehumanize themselves. It is, in the words of Karl Marx, a process of 'spiritual self-castration', of self-prostitution. Thus while the present economic system promotes conspicuous consumption among a few, it condemns the many to a stunted, crippled existence.

We have already noted that the masses are not the ones who set goals for economic activity. They have no control over the system, which, however, can maintain itself only with their sweat and blood. It is not they who decide what to produce, where to set up factories or how to distribute the products. They are thus reduced to being mere by-products of the system. They are not subjects of history but its objects. As objects they are formed or deformed by the privileged classes, who alone hold in their hands the reins of the economy. This is a process that goes on both inside and outside the place of work. In the place of work the natural and spontaneous needs of the working class find no outlet and therefore atrophy. All their needs are reduced to the need for wages. Even this minimal need goes unfulfilled. For the wage structure is determined not by the quantum of service one renders to society but by certain unjust criteria inherited from the past. One such criterion is the superiority of intellectual over manual work, which is to be traced back to the caste-ridden feudal system in which the Brahmins, in virtue of their monopoly over learning, also enjoyed economic and social privileges. Yet another criterion is the amount one has invested towards receiving training or initiating enterprises. But it is all too often forgotten that such investments were made possible by unjust laws of inheritance. Thus one injustice is used to justify another.[9]

To sum up, the present economic system is essentially unjust. It expropriates from the mass of producers not only the products of work but also the means of production. It condemns them to what is equivalent to slave labour. It denies them the possibility of creating their own future, of shaping their own destiny. The reverse

side of this economic servitude is social fragmentation
and inequality, whose main elements we shall now dis-
cuss.

Man Divided

The social fetters the Indian masses have to break are
of two types: those originating in feudalism and those
others created by the capitalist mode of production.

CASTE INEQUALITY

The traditional form of caste is still a force to be reck-
oned with, especially in rural India. We have a pointer to
it in the not too infrequent newspaper reports about the
burning of Harijans by caste Hindus in different parts of
the country. But, on the whole, caste has undergone a
significant change in recent decades. The vertical solidarity of caste based on ritual superiority has largely disin-
tegrated. In its place a new horizontal solidarity is taking
shape as a result of the joining together of various sub-
castes which traditionally fought one another. This form
of solidarity has become a source of economic and political power where it enjoys numerical strength. It has led
to the emergence of the so-called dominant castes like
the Nairs of Kerala, the Gounders, Padayachis, and
Mudaliars of Tamil Nadu, the Lingayath and Okaligas of
Karnataka, the Kammas and the Reddis of Andhra
Pradesh, the Marathas of Maharashtra, the Patidars of
Gujarat, the Jats, Ahirs, Rajputs, and Kayasthas of
Northern India.[10]

The dominant castes have a vested interest in maintaining the economic backwardness of the lower castes
and the outcasts. They control most of the Panchayats
and government agencies for rural development. For
instance, in Andhra Pradesh the Panchayat Samitis consists almost entirely of the dominant landowning

castes.[11] What makes the situation still worse is the fact that often the dominant castes and the exploiting classes are the same people. From the ranks of the former are drawn a large percentage of the landlords, moneylenders, merchants, industrialists, and bureaucrats. It is the members of the dominant castes who, with the connivance of government officials, appropriate the greater part of the resources set apart for the uplift of the poor.[12]

CLASS EXPLOITATION

More iniquitous than caste inequality is the class exploitation introduced by the capitalist system. In the industrial sector the main agents of exploitation are the big businessmen and entrepreneurs who monopolize the means of production and exploit human labour solely for profit. Then come the commercial elite, who have been playing an increasingly dominant role in Indian economic life. Instead of using money capital for productive use, they indulge in hoarding, in blackmarketing, and in creating artificial scarcity with a view to maximizing profit.[13] In relation to these oppressor classes, independent professionals such as doctors, lawyers, and engineers play a supportive role. They depend very much on the patronage of the industrial and commerical community. The large majority of technicians and applied scientists trained in India or elsewhere look to businessmen as their potential or actual employers, whose interests, consequently, they are forced to protect.[14] The urban privileged classes have entered into a sort of tacit alliance, on the one hand, with the bureaucrats and the politicians, and, on the other, with the rural elite.

Among the exploiting classes in rural areas we may mention, first of all, the feudal type of landowners who still survive in many parts of India—absentee landlords and peasant landlords. Next come the moneylenders

who charge exorbitant interest rates and in case of de-
fault of payment dispossess the debtors of their
property.[15] Still a third exploiting section in the rural
areas consists of merchants and middlemen. After every
harvest they buy up the agricultural produce at very low
prices and resell them at higher rates. They naturally ally
themselves with the landlords and the moneylenders.
Often the same people play the roles of moneylender,
merchant, and landlord.

Community of interests has created a close bond of
mutual support and collaboration between the rural and
the urban elite. The urban capitalists find in rich peasants
and landlords not only buyers of conspicuous consumption goods but also suppliers of the necessary raw mater-
ials for industrial production. Like the urban, the rural
elite function in close collaboration with bureaucrats and
politicians. Their oppressive hold on the rural population consisting of small peasants, landless workers, and
ruined artisans is tightening every day.[16]

It follows from our analysis that there exists in India an
axis of oppression constituted by the rural and urban
elite as well as by bureaucrats and politicians. This axis
has to be broken if the masses are to achieve economic
freedom and social equality.

Power Versus People

An oppressive socio-economic system can beget only
an oppressive state. Exploitation at the level of economic
and social life finds its support, sanction, and legitimacy
in the political system. The Indian State, whether we
consider it in its legislative, executive, or judicial functions, has become the enemy number one of the people.

Political power today is vested in the privileged classes. This has been the case right from independence when
power was transferred by the British to the Indian

National Congress, which alone had sufficient organiza-
tional basis and popular appeal. The backbone of the
party consisted of the educated middle class, which, in
spite of the vague socialist ideology of its leaders, was
deeply committed to the defence of private property.
This class bias has since then become accentuated, and is
vitiating the legislative, executive, and judicial functions
of the State.

Let us first consider legislation. Only the members of
the dominant castes or classes are in a position to stand
as candidates for election to the legislative bodies
whether in the states or at the centre. They alone have
the financial resources to meet election expenses, which
often run to lakhs of rupees. They alone have the benefit
of the higher education needed both for election propaganda and for fulfilling their role in the legislatures. In
order to win votes they exploit the feudal and economic
backwardness of the people. Where feudal attitudes of
hierarchy and personal loyalty prevail, the rich candi-
date can count on the votes of the masses, especially in
rural areas. Where such attitudes have died out, he can
still buy votes or extort them through various kinds of
intimidation. Consequently, the state and central legislatures are dominated and controlled by the privileged
classes. For instance in West Bengal, rural leadership in
the legislative assembly consists of people from the
upper income groups.[17] The poor candidates look to big
merchants and businessmen for election funds, which
the latter willingly provide since thereby they can influence political decisions. Thus economic power goes
hand in hand with political power.[18]

Since the class structure of the legislatures weighs
heavily in favour of the rich it would be vain to expect the
so-called representatives of the people to bring about the
necessary amendments to the Constitution or pass pro-

gressive economic and social laws. That would be expecting them to cut off the very branch on which they are comfortably seated. In public they mouth socialist slogans but in private they identify themselves with the exploiters of the people. This judgement applies also to the political parties. Not the good of the masses but lust for power and money is the mainspring of political activity today.

The same class bias also vitiates the judiciary. This is true not only of the system of laws in terms of which justice is administered but also in terms of those who administer the law. The Constitution and the law reflect the interests of those who framed them, namely, the upper and the middle classes. Besides, the legal system itself is a relic of colonialism and is unsuited to the needs of a developing country. It was formulated to maintain stability rather than to promote change. Since the existing social order is unjust, the laws that seek to perpetuate it are equally unjust. Finally, the very class composition of the judiciary renders it a useless instrument for the administration of justice to all. The judges on the whole come from the urban elite, whose ideology and interests they naturally share. What is worse, the very persons entrusted with the administration of justice resort to corrupt practices. An official committee appointed by the Government reported in 1964 that corruption exists in the lower ranks of the judiciary all over India, and that in some places it has spread to the higher ranks also.[19]

Finally, the masses are kept ignorant of their legal rights and this ignorance is exploited by the privileged classes and the bureaucracy. Even when their rights are manifestly flouted, the people are unable to move the court and get justice done. They are barred from doing so by the corrupt practice of lawyers who demand exorbitant fees for their professional service. In such conditions, to have recourse to the court is equal to opting for economic suicide. If in despair the people take the law into their own hands the iron hand of the police and the army come down upon them in the name of justice! Legal justice in our country is an article of conspicuous consumption which only the very rich can afford.

Much of what we have said about the judiciary applies equally well to the bureaucracy as a whole. The Indian bureaucracy has become largely disfunctional in respect of the promotion of justice and economic development. It has to function within the framework of rigid rules and regulations inherited from the British. Where these are strictly adhered to, they pose insuperable obstacles before the common man. Bureaucracy suffers also from overcentralization, making it impossible for lower officials to make responsible decisions. The farther removed from the social base is the centre of decision the greater is the delay involved and the less adequate the decisions taken. In fact the bureaucratic system has become almost autonomous vis-à-vis the people. Responsibility not towards the people but towards higher officials or to the impersonal system is what determines the conduct of officials. These inherent defects are aggravated by the class composition of the bureaucracy. Eighty percent of the officers in the Indian Administrative Service, the Indian Foreign Service, and the Indian Police Service are drawn from the top ten percent of the population, i.e., from the privileged classes to whom they are in loyalty bound. Officials use their discretionary power in favour of the big businessmen whom they consider as potential employers of their sons and daughters. Not infrequently they themselves, on retirement, seek employment in big business.[20] Assimilated within the exploiting classes, the bureaucracy has also assumed the characteristics of a caste. They are what the Brahmins were in traditional

India, and before them the common people sink to the level of untouchables. They have only rights and no obligations in relation to the people, who, on the contrary, have only obligations and no rights!

For government officials corruption has become almost a way of life. According to the report of the same official committee referred to earlier, in all transactions on behalf of the government a regular percentage is received by officials in the form of bribes that they share among themselves in agreed proportions. In the constructions of the Public Works Department the amount received is anything between seven to eleven percent.[21] Such appropriation of public funds must be viewed against the background of the fact that the greater part of the revenue of each state is paid out to government officials in the form of salary. Seen from this angle the bureaucracy is the cancer of the body politic.

If the state in its legislative, executive, and judicial functions is geared to the promotion of the interests of the privileged classes, it can in no true sense of the term be called democratic. What we have in reality is a form of classocracy, i.e., a government of, by, and for the privileged classes.

Ideological Fetters

The present oppressive social system finds an accomplice in ideology. By ideology we mean the system of ideas and values that determine the pattern of behaviour of a people. Ideology in India is a complex reality and is going through a period of crisis caused by the transition from feudalism to capitalism. While feudal ideas and

---

In writing this part of the chapter, the author has drawn largly upon his article, "Values in Crisis" in *Jeevadhara* 27 (Jan–Feb. 1975), pp. 12–23.

values are either dying out or assuming a new content, those of capitalism are on the ascendant. Ideology, whether feudalist or capitalist, acts as an obstacle to progress by legitimizing the status quo and thereby dampening the spontaneous urge of the masses to revolt against it.

THE LEGACY OF FEUDALISM

In the sphere of religious beliefs there is, first of all, the traditional emphasis on the pursuit and realization of the spiritual in man. Underlying this mentality is a dualist conception of man as a soul imprisoned in a body. Liberation (*mukti*) here means liberation of the soul from the body. Since the body is the principle of man's solidarity with the material world and of his insertion into the flux of time, liberation necessarily demands flight from the world of time and space, from the course of history. A sort of dualism is discernable even in Advaita, which claims to be nondualist, inasmuch as it enjoins on man to supercede the realm of empirical truth and attain to that of the transcendental truth. Naturally where such attitudes prevail there is an inevitable devaluation of all temporal activities, whether economic, social, political, or cultural.

More than the dualist mode of thinking, it is belief in karma and samsara that functions as opium for the people. The doctrine of karma could be understood in a positive sense as signifying the vocation of man to create his own future through the right mode of action. Quite different, however, is the popular understanding of it as the inevitable and necessary working out here and now of one's deeds in a previous life. Viewed from this angle, it breeds fatalism, pessimism, and resignation. The same attitudes find further nourishment in the sacral conception of the world, which sees every aspect of life as governed by rules and taboos ordained and sanctioned by the gods.

Similarly, undue stress on individual salvation and the total absence of any idea of collective destiny stand in the way of the emergence of a social humanism, which alone could provide an adequate basis for a truly socialist society. Individualism reigns also in the domain of morality. The primary moral concern is the practice of personal virtues such as austerity, self-control, detachment, and chastity and not man's social obligations.

The masses are held in bondage also by certain traditional social attitudes and values which serve either to reinforce the capitalist system or to smother the urge to revolt against it. Psychologically attuned to the collectivism of the traditional institutions of joint-family and caste, both of which subordinated the individual to the group, the people have little difficulty in adapting themselves to the collectivism of firms and factories. They find it natural to work for goals in the choice of which they have no say. Centuries of psychological conditioning by caste hierarchy facilitate transition to the hierarchy of functions and authority inherent in capitalist production. Accustomed to considering wealth and status as associated with birth, the working class sees nothing unjust in seeing a few people concentrating in their hands the means of agricultural and industrial production. The division of labour characteristic of the caste system finds a counterpart in the capitalist division of labour. Traditional conceptions regarding the superiority of Brahmins as repositories of knowledge and bearers of economic privileges dovetail with the capitalist assumption of the superiority of intellectual over manual labour. Thus through a process of transference, feudal attitudes and values go to reinforce capitalism, at least in its initial stages of development. Finally, loyalties derived from kinship, caste, and community divide the exploited masses into so many opposing groups that they become unable to present a common front against the guardians and legitimizers of the existing social system.

THE VIRUS OF CAPITALISM

Deprived of its economic base, feudal ideology is either dying out or undergoing profound internal changes. Not so the capitalist system of ideas and values, since it is firmly rooted in an ever-expanding system of the capitalist mode of production. Hence it poses a greater threat to the true development of man than the vestiges of feudal ideology.

The fundamental value of capitalism is private interest, which has its economic basis in private property. Private interest implies a negation of the social dimension of man, inasmuch as it reduces society to a mere means to individual ends. Where it reigns supreme, one's neighbour takes on the character of either a threat or a rival. The threat has to be eliminated, the rival overcome. Thus competition becomes the order of the day. In any competition only he can survive who asserts himself aggressively. In consequence, force, whether physical, moral, or psychological, becomes socially respectable, and the law of the survival of the fittest determines economic life. Within this frame of reference freedom means the chances a person has to pursue his individual ends unhindered by others. In reality such freedom amounts to licence for the few to exploit the many. Similarly, equality in capitalism resembles the 'equal' opportunity that physically unequal competitors have in a race. It is a type of equality in which some are more equal than others.

Private interest manifests itself in the pursuit of profit and in production for the sake of profit. As a result, production and efficiency rank high in the system of values. Production may become even an autonomous value where it is viewed as a symbol of social power. Usually it is geared to profit, and profit to consumption. The end-result is consumerism in the form of the fever for more and more comforts, more and more gadgets. With this a new concept of happiness emerges. A person's happiness consists in having something which his neighbour does not have, and his unhappiness in not having something which the latter has. His value is judged in terms of what he *has* and not what he *is*. And he can have whatever he wants if he has money. Thus money becomes the mother of all values, the value of all values.

It is this system of values that is the principal determinant of economic, social, and political life in contemporary India. From the upper classes it is percolating to the lower classes; from the urban areas it is spreading to the rural. It is being progressively internalized by the masses. However, this process is not always a spontaneous one; it is largely manipulated. To sell their products the capitalists artificially generate needs in the people. This is done with the help of advertisements, posters, exhibitions, and the like. To this end they prostitute sex, womanhood, family, religion, and even God. They weave myths around commodities and project them as symbols of status. Thus the economic system produces not only consumption goods but also consumer classes.

The values of capitalism have shaped the minds of people to such an extent that even when they revolt they do so in the name of these same values. The student agitations in the country, for instance, are not so much against the capitalist system as against their being denied the benefits of the same system. So too it is largely private interest that motivates strikes and demonstrations on the part of the organized working class. What is still more distressing is that even political parties professing socialism have become infected with the virus of capitalist ideology. Most politicians and legislators representing left-view politics do so merely as a means for promoting their economic interests. Thus we have the paradox of Communists fighting capitalism in the name of capitalist values.

It follows from the foregoing analysis that the Indian masses can achieve liberation only through a total revolution, consisting in a restructuring of both society and ideology. What is needed is nothing less than the creation of a new society in which the human person will be the highest value, one in which the good of all will consist in the full flowering of each individual, in which cooperation will replace competition, love will replace aggression, quality will have primacy over quantity, the aesthetic will subsume the useful. It will have to be a society in which freedom will be realized not in spite of, but through one's fellowmen, in which commodities will take on the character of gifts, and the materialism of consumption will be replaced by the humanism of communion.

The Bondage Within

Thus far we have considered only those forms of human bondage which affect society as a whole and enjoy a certain autonomy in relation to individuals. There are also others, which affect individuals in the deepest core of their existence, such as ignorance regarding the ultimate meaning of life, the ambivalence and vulnerability of freedom with its concomitants of sin and guilt, and finally, the problem of survival after death.

Besides, there are psychic determinants in the form of subconscious or unconscious forces that curtail man's ability to determine his own future. These problems are largely part of what we may call the human condition and, as such, are universal. No man, to whichever historical stage or culture he belongs, is exempt from them. The rich as well as the poor, the exploiter as well as the exploited, the educated as well as the illiterate, have to come to terms with them at one time or other in their lives. However, there are periods of historical crisis when these problems make themselves particularly felt. Our country is witnessing the initial stages of such a crisis of culture.

Unfortunately, too little research has been done in this field to enable us to make valid generalizations. All that can be said is that these existential problems do exist and are experienced differently by different people, depending on whether they belong to the urban or rural areas, to the affluent or to the middle and poorer classes. One thing seems certain: It is neither the extreme rich nor the extreme poor but the middle classes—more precisely, the middle-class youth—that are today raising questions regarding the deepest problems of human existence. The very poor still cling to solutions offered by the traditional world-outlook and religious beliefs. The very rich, on the contrary, are caught up in the initial euphoria of consumerism, and are not yet disillusioned enough with it to pose questions regarding life and death. Contrasted with these, the middle-class youth have neither safe moorings in the past nor security regarding the future. It is they who are gripped by the problems of a culture in transition. Even among them it is only a minority that succeeds in articulating what their peers experience existentially.

However that may be, with the progressive disintegration of traditional culture, the existential problems of man are likely to become more and more accentuated. They have to be taken seriously for the following reasons: First, they are in themselves expressions of man's estrangement from his true being, from what he ought to be. Second, they contribute in their own way to the perpetuation of the unjust social system and even give birth to ever-new forms of the oppression of man by man. The creation of a new society is not possible without creating anew the minds and hearts of man.

The challenge of integral liberation in India, of which we have tried to describe the salient features, is one that confronts all the citizens of the country, to whichever creed, community, or political party each one belongs. It is also one that calls for unconditional commitment. All those who do not refuse to be their brothers' keeper are asking themselves how they may respond to the challenge in the light of their own total vision of man. The disciples of Jesus are likewise bound to ask: What answer does Jesus give to the historic challenge of the total liberation of the Indian masses? Does his answer meet the needs of today? In what respects is it in need of revision and reinterpretation? What follows is an attempt at answering these questions.

NOTES

1. Meghnad Desai, "India: Contradictions of Slow Capitalist Development," in *Explosion in a Subcontinent*, ed. Robin Blackburn (London: Penguin, 1975), pp. 28–30.

2. V. M. Dandekar and Nilakantha Rath, *Poverty in India* (Bombay: Krishna Raj, 1971), pp. 31–33.

3. *Ibid.*, p. 68.

4. Desai, "India: Contradictions," p. 29.

5. *Ibid.*, p. 19.

6. Gunnar Myrdal, *Asian Drama: An Inquiry into the Poverty of Nations*, 3 vols. (New York: Pantheon, 1968), II, p. 819.

7. Mansur Hoda, ed., *Problems of Unemployment in India* (Bombay: Allied Publishers, 1972), p. 26.

8. Dandekar and Rath, *Poverty in India*, pp. 124–26.

9. D. R. Gadgil, *Planning and Economic Policy in India* (Poona: Grokkale Institute of Politics and Economics, 1974), p. 97.

10. M. N. Srinivas, *Caste in Modern India, and Other Essays* (New York: Asia Publishing House, 1974), p. 90.

11. Hugh Gray, "The Problem," in *Rural Sociology in India*, ed. A. R. Desai (Bombay: Popular Prakasan, 1969), p. 537.

12. Myrdal, *Asian Drama*, I, p. 286.

13. Joost Kuitenbrouwer, *Growth and Equality in India and China: A Comparative Analysis* (The Hague: Institute of Social Studies, 1973), p. 7.

14. Gadgil, *Planning*, p. 308.

15. Myrdal, *Asian Drama*, II, p. 1057.

16. M. N. Srinivas, "Changing Attitudes in India Today," *Yojana* (Delhi), Oct. 1961.

17. Miron Weiner, "Political Leadership in West Bengal," in *Rural Sociology in India*, p. 733.

18. Gadgil, *Planning*, p. 306.

19. *Report of the Santhanam Committee*, I (New Delhi: Government of India, 1964), p. 108.

20. Gadgil, *Planning*, p. 306.

21. *Report of the Santhanam Committee*, I, p. 10.

III

The Prophet of the New Humanity

Historically, all religions have played a role in society either by protesting against its evils or providing it with norms and sanctions. This is particularly true of the religion of the Hebrews, since they regarded God as revealing himself primarily in historical events and situations. Originally the focus of their faith was the past intervention of God in liberating them from slavery in Egypt and leading them to the Promised Land flowing with milk and honey. In course of time, with the emergence of prophecy, the emphasis shifted from the past to the future, namely, to the definitive intervention of God in the end-time. This did not, however, mean that the prophets ignored the actual problems of society. On the contrary. The more intense their longing for the future, the more vehement was also their criticism of social evils. For, in their view, the future had meaning only as the final overcoming of the evils of the present. Thus, in the great prophets—Hosea, Micah, Isaiah, and Jeremiah—the expectation of the future and the denunciation of the status quo draw nourishment from each other and combine to form but one powerful religious current. It is in the line of these great prophets that Jesus stands.

And it is his mission as a prophet that is of particular

relevance for us today. For prophecy is not a thing of the past but an essential dimension of individual and collective life in all stages of history. When we revolt against whatever is dehumanizing and commit ourselves to the construction of a worthier future for man we are doing what the prophets did of old. There is therefore no surer common ground between us and Jesus than prophecy. Unfortunately, Christian tradition from very early times devalued the prophet in Jesus and thereby obscured what was most challenging and significant in his life and teaching. Now the time has come to reaffirm the centrality of his prophetic role as attested by the Synoptic Gospels themselves.

The Prophet from Nazareth

That he claimed to be a prophet is beyond doubt. Unable to work miracles in his own hometown because of the unbelief of its folk, he complained, not without a tinge of sadness: "A prophet will always be held in honour except in his hometown, and among his kinsmen and family" (Mark 6:4). He claimed to possess the Spirit of God, which in his days was taken as a mark of the prophetic call (Luke 4:18). As his life unfolded with all its tensions and conflicts it became increasingly clear to him that like the prophets of old he too would be put to death. Hence his reply to the Pharisees who came to advise him to flee from Herod who was out to kill him: "I must be on my way today and tomorrow and the next day, because it is unthinkable for a prophet to meet his death anywhere but in Jerusalem" (Luke 13:32).

His disciples too took him to be a prophet. Soon after his ignominious death on the cross two of them spoke of him as a "prophet powerful in speech and action before God and the whole people" (Luke 24:19). It was as a prophet that he was recognized by the common people.

Those who saw him raise the widow's son to life could not but exclaim: "A great prophet has arisen among us" (Luke 7:16). Same was the reaction of the crowd when he entered Jerusalem: "This is the prophet Jesus, from Nazareth in Galilee" (Matt. 21:11).

As a prophet his mission was to confront his contemporaries with the will of God as revealed in history, and to call upon them to respond to its demands through a personal decision.

The New Humanity

What was the divine purpose he saw inscribed in history? The answer is contained in the central theme of his message as recorded by Mark: "The time has come; the kingdom of God is upon you; repent, and believe the Gospel" (Mark 1:15). As is to be expected, Jesus does not give us any systematic exposition of what he meant by the kingdom of God. However, his teaching contains sufficient data on the basis of which we can describe its salient features. The Sermon on the Mount is particularly revealing:

> How blest are those who know their need of God;
> the kingdom of Heaven is theirs.
> How blest are the sorrowful;
> they shall find consolation.
> How blest are those of a gentle spirit;
> they shall have the earth for their possession.
> How blest are those who hunger and thirst to see right prevail;
> they shall be satisfied.
> How blest are those who show mercy;
> mercy shall be shown to them.
> How blest are those whose hearts are pure;
> they shall see God.
> How blest are the peacemakers;
> God shall call them his sons.

How blest are those who have suffered persecution for the
  cause of right;
  the kingdom of Heaven is theirs (Matt. 5:3–10).

An attentive reading of this passage will show that the
structure and movement of Jesus' thinking reflects that
of our basic human experience, which is essentially ambivalent. All our experience is at once negative and positive: negative, inasmuch as it reveals elements that di-
minish our knowing, thinking, and being; positive, inasmuch as it contains elements of truth, beauty, and
goodness. At least implicitly we reject the former and
affirm the latter, and that too in an absolute manner.
Rejection and affirmation are but two sides of the same
coin. The rejection of evil *is* the affirmation of the good.
Both are instinct with hope, are themselves acts of hope.
We live in the hope that we shall overcome the evil and
realize the good. This hope is the background against
which our life unfolds. It is this absolute horizon of hope
that Jesus had in mind when he spoke of the kingdom of
God, with this difference, that for him its realization was
not only a possibility but also a certainty, not only a
project but also a promise.

  In the Sermon on the Mount he proclaimed that God
will come to root out whatever is opposed to the fullness
of man—sorrow, injustice, and estrangement from himself. He will come to affirm and fulfill whatever is truly
human—gentleness of spirit, concern for right, purity of
heart, commitment or peace, mercy to one's fellowmen.
The kingdom of God therefore is, on the one hand, the
liberation of man from every alienation, i.e., from everything that renders him other than what he ought to be,
and on the other, the full flowering of the human on our
planet. In other words, it is not only freedom *from* but
also freedom *for*—freedom for creativity, community,
and love.

Seen from another angle, the kingdom may be described as the definitive reconciliation of man with nature, with other persons, with God, and with himself. Its coming means that man will take possession of the earth. As lord of the earth he will no more be subject to blind cosmic forces. Created anew, the earth will put forth all its riches at the service of man. Everything around him, whether already given or refashioned by him, will be a symbol and instrument of human togetherness instead of being tools in the hands of some to exploit others. In the kingdom man will rejoin his fellowmen. Reconstituted sons of God, every man will be a brother to his neighbour. His need for his kind, for love and recognition of others, will be fully satisfied. The New Age will thus mark the end of inequality, injustice, and exploitation. The realization of universal love will be at the same time man's final reconciliation with God. In communal love man will meet God, and in meeting God discover his oneness with all. Rooted in God, each man will achieve unity, harmony, and peace with himself. In the language of the Seer, God "will wipe away every tear from their eyes; there shall be an end to death, and to mourning and crying and pain; for the old order has passed away" (Rev. 21:3–4).

The Not–Yet and the Already

When Jesus spoke of the reign of God he did not mean by that term the action of God whereby he brought the world into being and maintains it in existence. He, of course, believed, as every Jew did, that the world owes its origin to God, that it is he who feeds the birds of the air and clothes the lilies of the field. Jesus had something else in mind when he announced that the reign of God was at hand. He meant that God was going to intervene *definitively* in history to sum it up and bring it to fulfillment. His eyes were focused on the future of the human community, not on just any future but on the absolute future free even from the possibility of alienation.

It was this hope in the future as absolute freedom that he expressed in symbolic language when he said:"Many, I tell you, will come from east and west to feast with Abraham, Isaac, and Jacob in the kingdom of Heaven" (Matt. 8:11). He wanted his disciples too to plant their gaze on the kingdom yet to come. This is borne out by the nature of the prayer he taught them. If the disciples asked their master to teach them to pray it was not because they did not know how. Every Jew did. The real motive was their desire for a prayer that would express their distinctive faith as *his* disciples as distinguished from other religious sects who had their own distinctive prayers. It is significant that the prayer they were taught had for its central motif the coming of the reign of God: "Father, thy name be hallowed; thy kingdom come" (Luke 11:2). The disciples are called not to sit around their master and enjoy his company, but to look forward to the coming reign of God. They are to march with him to meet the God who is about to arrive.

Though the reign of God as a future event was the primary concern of Jesus it would be wrong to conclude that for him that future began where our history ended. The age of freedom is not something that comes to fill the vacuum created by the death of our age, by the disappearance of our world. Rather, the future he looked forward to was seen by him as already present, though only germinally, in the *here* and *now* of his experience. He saw the future as impinging on the present, as a new and different dawn over the realities of history. To put it differently, he saw the present not as something closed in and rounded off in itself but as open to the future and its fullness, as pregnant with promises for the full revelation of man and God.

What was that present in which he saw the irruption of the future? It was above all, his own present, his own presence in word and deed. "But if it is by the finger of God that I drive out the devils, then be sure the kingdom of God has already come upon you" (Luke 11:20).[1] He saw God at work in the exorcisms and cures he performed. To the messengers of John who approached him with the query whether he was 'the one who is to come' or some other, he answered: "Go and tell John what you have seen and heard: how the blind recover their sight, the lame walk, the lepers are made clean, the deaf hear, the dead are raised to life, the poor are hearing the good news—and happy is the man who does not find me a stumbling-block" (Luke 7:22–23). Whether Jesus believed himself to be the 'one who is to come' is a moot question. But it is beyond doubt that he saw in the cures he worked so many signs of God's saving presence. In and through his word and deed the reign of God became a matter of human experience. This seems to be the meaning of his saying: ". . . for in fact the kingdom of God is among you" (Luke 17–21).[2]

Jesus used many and varied symbols to express the germination of the new age in the womb of the old. The light of the age to come shines forth and dispels darkness whenever the disciples do good to their fellowmen who, seeing it, praise their Father in heaven (Matt. 5:14–16). The wine of the New Age is already active and is bursting the bounds of the old wineskin of Judaism (Mark 2:22). Just as a pinch of salt sprinkled over food purifies and preserves it, the creative power of the kingdom purifies the world and preserves what is good and true in it (Matt. 5:13). It is active in history in the manner of the little yeast that leavens a huge quantity of dough (Matt. 13:33). Again, God's reign is "like the mustard-seed, which is smaller than any seen in the ground at its sowing. But once sown, it springs up and grows taller than any other plant, and forms branches so large that the birds can settle in its shade" (Mark 4:31–32). The seeds of the future are breaking the soil, putting forth leaves and bearing fruit. And the harvest of the end-time is already begun (Mark 4:4–8).

Did Jesus think of the reign of God as present exclusively in his own mighty word and deed? No. We already saw that the light of the kingdom shines forth through the conduct of the disciples. It is radiated by all those who come to the aid of their brothers in need. This is the deeper truth contained in the parable of the Good Samaritan. The New Humanity is present wherever man lovingly reaches out to his neighbour, wherever there is concern and responsibility for one another, wherever men and women gather together to share what they are and what they have, and, in their togetherness, experience oneness with the ultimate ground of all. The visage of the New Age may be discerned wherever the blind see, the deaf hear, the lame walk, the leper is rendered whole, the prisoners set free, the unloved receive love, and the hopeless regain hope. It announces his presence wherever fetters are broken and man-made walls are demolished to let each man be all men.

A Gift and a Task

How will the New Age come into being? Will it be the fruit solely of the action of God? Or solely of human endeavour? Or will it be the work of both God and man? These are the questions to which we shall address ourselves now.

That Jesus conceived the New Humanity as a gift from

God, none may doubt. The very term 'reign of God' means primarily the action of God whereby he brings everything under his dominion. This aspect of Jesus' message is particularly stressed in the Beatitudes as recorded by Luke. There, participation in the blessings of the New Age presupposes nothing more than the vacuum of human need, the vacuum of poverty, hunger, sorrow, and infamy (Luke 6:20–22). The same truth finds expression in the words: "Let the children come to me, do not try to stop them; for the kingdom of God belongs to such as these" (Mark 10:14). What is held up here for imitation is not the humility and the innocence of children, but their being receptive and expecting everything from the bounty and goodness of others. Only those have access to the kingdom who expect everything from God and cast all their hopes on him. Man cannot construct the New Humanity solely with his own resources. He can only sow the seeds of the New Age. It is up to God to make them grow and frucitify. "The kingdom of God is like this. A man scatters seed on the land; he goes to bed at night and gets up in the morning, and the seed sprouts and grows—how, he does not know. The ground produces a crop by itself, first a blade, then the ear, then full-grown corn in the ear; but as soon as the crop is ripe, he plies the sickle, because the harvest-time has come" (Mark 4:26–29). The same truth underlies Jesus' teaching on prayer. The disciples can do no more than pray, 'Thy kingdom come'. But to come and reveal himself—that is a matter of the free decision of God.

To understand the deeper meaning of the gift character of the kingdom an analogy from ordinary human experience may help. A young boy meets a girl. He eventually develops a liking for her. And in course of time liking grows into love. He expresses his new-born love in many a fashion—through looks, gestures, words, gifts, and so on. Yet he knows full well that none of his initiatives can necessarily make her love him in return. If she does reciprocate it is not a necessary outcome of his attentions but a free self-giving. Nothing less than a free gift on her part can transform their relationship into a true communion, into the nucleus of a community. Similarly, humankind cannot merit or take possession of God through its own efforts. If every love is a gift, such preeminently is God's love for man. The love whereby he gathers humanity into his heart can therefore only be a gift born of infinite freedom.

Does this mean that all man has to do for the coming of the New Age is to remain quiet and do nothing? Has human initiative and commitment no relevance for the realization of the New Humanity? Not at all. The message of the New Age as a gratuitous gift of God has for its reverse side the call for human response. Jesus demands from his disciples active response in the form of faith and repentance (Mark 1:15). Repentance here means something more than mere expression of sorrow for past sins. It consists rather in a reorientation of one's whole life, with the implied acceptance of new norms and goals. It calls for a qualitative change in one's system of values and mode of life. If the community itself is the subject of repentance, the adequate response can be nothing less than a restructuring of the entire social and cultural system. Those members of the community who choose to repent will consequently have to live in a situation of conflict and tension with those who do not. This explains why the disciples of Jesus had to face opposition from the religious establishment.

The need for man's response comes into clearer relief in the Matthaean formulation of the Beatitudes. Unlike Luke, Matthew makes entry into the kingdom conditional upon man's showing mercy to his kind, his being an instrument of peace in the community, keeping his heart pure, and hungering and thirsting for justice (Matt. 5:7–9). Of all, the most important prerequisite is love, a love that is more than mere wishing well, a love that must show itself in doing the will of the Father, in giving, in forgiving and, above all, in service (Matt. 7:21; 5:43–48; 6:14; Mark 10:42–45). It must take the form also of fighting the forces opposed to the reign of God. That was why Jesus sent his disciples not only to preach the good news but also to work cures and to cast out demons.

Clearly then, the coming of the New Age presupposes not only the initiative of God but also the obedient and creative participation of man. But how can it be at the same time a divine gift and a human task? Are these not mutually exclusive and incompatible? By no means. Deeper reflection will show that the character of the New Age as gift does not make it any less a human task. To grasp this we must return to our analogy of human love. We saw that the lover neither merited nor effected the love his beloved had for him. This love was a pure gift, present right from the beginning of their relationship. It was in fact the openness of the girl to the boy, which was in itself a preliminary self-giving, that emboldened him to shed his inhibitions. In other words, it was her incipient self-giving that made him capable of responding. It came to him like an invitation, a challenge, and a promise: an invitation to give himself further, a challenge to work out the possibilities inherent in their relationship, and a promise that his response will meet with success. In sum, her gift of love became for him a task to be accomplished.

So is the reign of God. It is God's self-giving embodied in things, events, persons, and experiences that lies at the root of man's response, individual and collective. It too comes to him in the form of an invitation, a challenge, and a promise: an invitation to leave behind all the safe moorings of the past and march forward, a challenge to break all fetters and construct the future and, finally, a promise that this striving will come to a successful issue. Thus God's self-giving in history becomes, for those whose hearts and minds are open, a moral task. The New Heaven and New Earth is something mankind has to create, not by its own resources but in response to the horizon of absolute hope, not in monologue but in dialogue with God.

Though Jesus believed that the New Age demands active human response the stress is, manifestly, on its being the work of God. He speaks of the 'coming' of the kingdom, of men 'entering' it or even 'possessing' it. But nowhere does he speak of it explicitly as something to be constructed by man. He does not call upon his disciples, in so many words, to commit themselves to its creation. How to explain this one-sidedness in the teaching of Jesus?

The reason can be none other than that Jesus lived two thousand years ago and shared the thought patterns of prescientific man. In that age men and women could not have thought of their collective future as something to be fashioned by human effort. The conditions for planning the future—science, technology, industrialization, collective production, transport, mass media, etc.—had not yet been realized. And what man at any given period of history cannot do he naturally attributes to God. And Jesus was no exception to this.

Living as we do in the scientific age, we cannot, should not, identify ourselves with every aspect of his world outlook. That would amount to living in the past and abdicating the present. And our age demands that we stress, more than Jesus or our forebears did, that the New Humanity is something we have to construct in response to God, who beckons us from beyond. To do so is to be creatively faithful to Jesus, the only mode of fidelity that does justice to his basic concern.

The Manifesto of Jesus

If Jesus preached the New Humanity reborn in freedom not merely as a divine gift but also as a task, the question naturally arises: How did he himself respond to the divine invitation? How did he fulfill the task of sowing and nurturing the seeds of the New Age? In the present context we shall confine ourselves to indicating the general tenor of his response. Luke narrates an event that takes us right into the heart of the matter.

> So he came to Nazareth, where he had been brought up, and went to the synagogue on the Sabbath as he regularly did. He stood up to read the lesson and was handed the scroll of the prophet Isaiah. He opened the scroll and found the passage which says:
> 'The spirit of the Lord is upon me because he has anointed me; he has sent me to announce good news to the poor, to proclaim release for prisoners and recovery of sight for the blind; to let the broken victims go free, to proclaim the year of the Lord's favour.'
> He rolled up the scroll, gave it back to the attendant, and sat down; and all eyes in the synagogue were fixed on him. He began to speak: 'Today', he said, 'in your very hearing this text has come true' (Luke 4:16–21).

Here we have what we may call the manifesto of Jesus, the clearest expression of what he understood to be his mission in life. His task was not only to announce the age of divine favour but also, and above all, 'to let the broken victims go free'. God's purpose in history had to be realized through human effort for the liberation of man. This involved for Jesus, as it does for all who share his faith and hope, saying no to everything that oppressed man, and yes to everything that accorded with the interests of the New Age of the andric fullness. This 'no' and 'yes' determined his whole life from the day the Spirit invaded his soul on the banks of the Jordan to the fateful day he met his destiny on the cross.

It remains for us now to see how Jesus translated his no and yes into word and deed. We shall begin with a consideration of his response to man's estrangement from nature.

NOTES

1. See Joachim Jeremias, *New Testament Theology* (New York: Scribner, 1971), p. 170. (Hereafter abbreviated NTT.)

2. See Norman Perrin, *Rediscovering the Teaching of Jesus* (London: SCM, and New York: Harper, 1967), pp. 68–74.

IV

Cosmic Freedom

Right from his emergence in prehistoric times man found himself defenseless and insecure before the hostile forces of nature, vulnerable to heat and cold, rain and storms, illness, death, and decay. His history till now has been one of collective striving to conquer nature, whether external or internal to him, and to wrest from it whatever he needed for warding off evils and perpetuating himself.

The birth of science and technology opened new possibilities for man to realize freedom from nature, though at the same time it fashioned new fetters for him. The conquest and humanization of nature still remains very much a task to be completed. Still, compared with us, those who lived in the prescientific age were much more at the mercy of hostile nature. It was in such an age that Jesus lived. As is to be expected, the approach of his contemporaries to natural evils was more mythicoreligious than rational or scientific. As we shall see presently, Jesus himself probably shared the same approach.

Man in Bondage to Satan

Jesus as portrayed in the Gospels was a man finely attuned to the world of man and things. He did not look at nature from the standpoint of one standing outside it and confronting it as an object. Rather he had a sense of kinship with the tangible and the visible. These flowed into him, into the innermost recesses of his being, as though by some mysterious symbiosis, but only to come out in the form of words, which too had the quality of things—the taste, smell, and colour of the objects around him.

He was particularly sensitive to the beautiful, to form and harmony. "Consider how the lilies grow in the fields; they do not work, they do not spin; and yet, I tell you, even Solomon in all his splendour was not attired like one of these" (Matt. 6:28–29). His very sensitivity to the beautiful heightened his awareness of whatever was ugly, of whatever was out of harmony with the well-being of man. He knew by a sort of empathy the sufferings his fellowmen endured at the hands of a hostile nature. He knew about those who work hard and find the load heavy, those who toil the whole night at fishing and yet catch nothing, those who are anxious for food and drink, and those who have to work to earn their keep. He knew about the seed sown on rocky soil, which sprouted quickly but only to wither away, about the darnel that chokes the wheat, and about the moth and rust that spoil hidden treasures. He spoke of the rain, flood, and wind that destroy houses, of storms that rock boats endangering the lives of many.[1]

In his journeyings through the length and breadth of Palestine he came face to face with the sufferings caused by illness, decay, and death. Among the people who came to him for succour there were victims of possession, leprosy, fever, paralysis, hemorrhage, blindness, dumbness, lameness, epilepsy, dropsy, deformation, and of many other diseases.[2]

What significance did Jesus attach to these evils which oppressed his fellowmen? For an answer we have to recall the cultural gulf that separates him from us. The frame of reference of his thinking and judging was far different from ours. To us illness, for instance, is a relatively simple phenomenon intelligible in itself on the basis of laws governing the bodily organism and its interaction with equally intelligible factors obtaining in the external universe. To Jesus, on the contrary, illness constituted a highly complex phenomenon with more than one dimension of meaning.

Cosmic evils like the ones enumerated above had for him, first of all, a demonic dimension of meaning. Though belief in demons played only an insignificant role in the religious history of the Hebrews, in course of time, probably under Persian influence, it became widely prevalent among the people. Illnesses of all kinds were attributed to demons. They were held responsible for natural phenomena injurious to man, like storms and floods. One attributed to them also the power to enter the souls of men and induce madness, moral blindness, and even disobedience to God.[3] Jesus probably shared this belief of his contemporaries. Luke narrates an incident which is particularly significant in this context. While he was teaching in a synagogue Jesus saw a woman possessed by a spirit that had crippled her for eighteen years. He healed her by word of mouth and by laying his hands on her. To the president of the synagogue who accused him of violating the Sabbath he replied: "Is there a single one of you who would not loose his ox or his donkey from the manger and take it out to water on the Sabbath? And here is a woman, a daughter of Abraham, who has been kept prisoner by Satan for eighteen long years: was it wrong for her to be freed from her bonds on the Sabbath?" (Luke 13:10–17). These words clearly show that Jesus viewed illness as caused by Satan. He seems to attribute even natural

happenings to the working of demonic forces. When the
disciples called for help for fear of their boat capsizing in
the storm, he rebuked the wind as if it were a demon. All
this proves that in this matter also he was very much a
product of his age.

Jesus did not see demons as so many agents of evil
working at cross purposes. He saw them as an organized
force under the supreme command of their leader,
Satan. (Cf. Luke: 10:17–18; Matt. 10:25.) That is why he
could speak of the kingdom of Satan as opposed to the
kingdom of God.

This brings us to the religious dimension in Jesus'
understanding of cosmic bondage. In his view illness
and other physical evils imply a condition of alienation
from God. He tells the paralytic: "My son, your sins are
forgiven. . . . stand up, take your bed and go home"
(Mark 2:5–11). Here liberation from sin coincides with
liberation from illness. However, it is doubtful whether
he ascribed illness and natural calamities to personal sin
as such. For, in the Gospel according to Luke, we hear
him say that if the tower fell and killed eighteen people at
Siloam it was not because they were more guilty than
others (Luke 13:1–5). It is therefore more likely that when
he attributes natural evils to sin, he has in mind not so
much personal sin as cosmic sin, that is, the condition of
man out of harmony with the will of God.

Between God and Satan stood man, defenseless and
helpless, a mere shadow of what he ought to be. How far
the sick and the possessed were from man as God originally willed! Familiar with the Pentateuch as he was,
Jesus knew for sure that God created man in his image
and likeness "to rule the fish in the sea, the birds of
heaven, the cattle, all wild animals on earth, and all
reptiles that crawl upon the earth" (Gen. 1:26). He also
knew about the divine command given to man that he

should "fill the earth and subdue it" (Gen. 1:28). What he saw around him instead were men and women reduced to the condition of slaves, slaves to illnesses of varied kinds and at the mercy of demonic powers. He saw them diminished in being and knowing, crippled in spirit and body. He was particularly sensitive to this human dimension of the problem.

Illness, possession, and similar evils constituted a human problem also in another sense. Those afflicted with them were looked upon as objects of the divine wrath, which they justly merited through their own misdeeds. Besides, were they not mere playthings, if not abodes, of demons? They had thus become physically, morally, and ritually impure, defiling anyone who came into contact with them. This was particularly true of lepers, who as early as in the time of Leviticus had to cry 'Unclean, unclean', and live apart outside the camp (Lev. 13:45–46). Besides, the sick and the possessed were barred from entering the temple of Jerusalem. They were in every sense rejected by the community of men.

Setting the Oppressed Free

The response of Jesus to man's cosmic bondage may be summed up in the words of Peter as recorded in the Acts of the Apostles:"God anointed him with the Holy Spirit and with power. He went about doing good and healing all who were oppressed by the devil, for God was with him" (Acts 10:38). His prophetic no took the form of miracles.

The Gospels record several healings and exorcisms, three raisings of the dead, and seven nature miracles. Under nature miracles come walking on water, cursing the fig-tree, finding the coin in the fish's mouth, Peter's miraculous catch, the stilling of the storm, the feeding in the wilderness, and the changing of water into wine.[4]

Are all these miracles historically true? For an answer we have to keep in mind the cultural environment in which Jesus lived. The people of his age were gifted with vivid and creative imagination, which was a fertile ground for legends and myths. They tended to enhance the greatness of their heroes by attributing to them all sorts of superhuman deeds. This the early Christian community did also to Jesus whom they believed to be the saviour of the world. The Gospel accounts of the miracles, therefore, are not to be taken as newspaper reports. What happened in reality became overlaid with legends and myths. However, it would be wrong to dismiss all the miracle stories in the Gospels as mere products of creative phantasy. There is no doubt that Jesus performed some miracles of healing and exorcism, though it is impossible to determine which among them are genuine. Much less certain are we whether the so-called nature miracles contain any historical nucleus.[5]

Jesus attached great importance to his works of healing and exorcising. He did not view them as peripheral to his mission. On the contrary, he went to the extent of summing up his entire mission in terms of them. To the Pharisees who came to warn him against Herod's plan to kill him, he said: "Listen: today and tomorrow I shall be casting out devils and working cures; on the third day I reach my goal" (Luke 13:31–32). It is clear from this that Jesus saw the working of miracles as an integral part of his mission, from which no earthly power could deter him. The same overriding concern expressed itself in the mission he entrusted to his disciples. He charged them not only to preach the good news but also to heal and to cast out devils. He gave them the power to tread underfoot snakes and scorpions and all the forces of the enemy (Mark 3:14–16, Matt. 10:7–8). And he rejoiced exceedingly when they came back to report their successes.

Why did he attach such importance to miracles? Because he saw in them so many instances of God's victory over the kingdom of Satan. When the disciples returned after their mission to tell him that even the devils submitted to them, he replied: "I watched how Satan fell, like lightning, out of the sky" (Luke 10:18). He saw in the cures and exorcisms he performed the inbreaking of the reign of God in the world. "If it is by the finger of God that I drive out the devils, then be sure the kingdom of God has already come upon you" (Luke 11:20).

It is important to note in this context that Jesus does not put himself in the centre of things. He does not claim the miracles to be manifestations of his own power. He attributes them to 'the finger of God', i.e. to the power of God. Neither does he demand faith in him as a prerequisite for working miracles.[6] In most instances he tells the beneficiaries: "Your faith has cured you" (Matt. 9:29; Mark 5:34; Luke 17:19). The implicit meaning is: God has responded to your faith and has healed you. He even explicitly mentions God as the object of faith: "Have faith in God" (Mark 11:20–22). Jesus himself comes into the picture only as the one in and through whom divine power is at work. In the words of Luke, "the power of the Lord was with him to heal the sick" (5:17). Miracles are therefore primarily God's response to man's faith. So too they are a sign of divine forgiveness. "My son, your sins are forgiven" (Mark 2:5). All this shows that for Jesus the miracles constituted God's victory not only over Satan and his kingdom but also over man's unbelief and unrepentance.

Does this mean that he regarded the victims of sickness and possession as no more than mere means, guinea pigs, used by God to manifest his power over Satan? Far from it. For the victory of God over Satan *is* man's freedom from the forces of evil. The end-result is man reborn from the condition of a slave to that of a son, man restored to inner harmony and at peace with himself. In sum, it is man rendered whole, no longer fragmented, no longer a shadow of what he ought to be: "Your faith has made you *whole*."

The wholeness of man, the fruit of the miracles, is also social. Miracles are the manifestation of God's redeeming power, of his liberating love. But how did his power and love reveal itself? Through the man, Jesus of Nazareth. To put it differently, it was in meeting him that the sick and the possessed experienced the power and the love of God. Through him the divine became a social reality. Where man reached out to succour his fellowmen, God was born. It is from this angle that we should see the tenderness and warmth with which Jesus reacted to the infirm and the oppressed. He told the mad man of Gerasa:"Go home to your own folk and tell them what the Lord in his *mercy* has done for you" (Mark 5:19). When he saw the widow of Nain accompanying the body of her only son to the grave 'his heart went out to her' (Luke 7:13). He was moved with compassion when he saw the large crowd on the lakeside without having anything to eat (Mark 8:2). His surrender to the Father overflowed into surrender to his brethren in need.

We have seen that illness and other maladies carried with them social ostracism. Miracles reversed the process. The sick and the possessed were reintegrated into society. Jesus saw to it that the social stigma was removed also legally. That is why he told the healed leper: "Go and show yourself to the priest, and make the offering laid down by Moses for your cleansing; that will certify the cure" (Mark 1:43–44).

God's reign as mediated by Jesus makes man free *from* all alien forces and free *for* wholeness, personal as well as social. The wholeness is, of course, only germinal and anticipatory and will come to full bloom only in the New Heaven and the New Earth.

The Mission to Heal and to Humanize

We have seen that Jesus attached great importance to the work of healing and exorcizing and that he wanted his disciples to do the same. But living as we are, two thousand years after him, we cannot fully identify ourselves either with his understanding of cosmic bondage or with his response to it. The challenge of illness and other natural calamities presents itself differently to us than it did to him. Hence the need to distinguish what is historically conditioned from what is perennially valid in his word and deed.

Jesus like any man of his time believed in the existence of devils as personal beings endowed with intelligence and will. This was but natural in those days when men did not know that illnessess and other evils had their own natural causes, intelligible in themselves and capable of being mastered through human resources. And what they did not know and could not master they naturally attributed to the working of supernatural forces. This we cannot do today, thanks to the power science and technology have placed at our disposal to discover and subdue the forces of nature. We cannot consequently share the belief in demons.

This does not imply that Jesus did not work any miracle. It only means that he was mistaken about the causes of the various maladies he had to deal with. That he healed them by a mere word or gesture cannot be doubted. But how to explain this fact? Is it not contrary to the laws of nature?

First of all, we must rid ourselves of the false notion that miracles are contrary to the laws of nature. They are effected essentially in accordance with the laws of nature, although realized in an exceptional manner. Viewed from this angle, man is essentially a worker of miracles. By his very nature he brings order and harmony into the universe around him. In the measure in which he is human, he fashions order out of disorder, cosmos out of chaos. He assembles scattered blocks of stones, pieces them together, and we have the miracle of a mansion. He gathers together the hues and colours strewn around him, forms them into a pattern, and we have the miracle of a painting. He takes old words, breathes new meaning into them, strings them into a garland of thought and feeling, and we have the miracle of a poem. He assembles pieces of metal and wood, moulds them into a whole, couples them with the currents of the air and energy, and we have the miracle of an aeroplane.

The greater the incandescence of the human spirit the greater is its capacity to mould the powers of the cosmos to house its dreams and visions. And what extraordinary miracles may we expect from a man whose spirit was taken hold of by the spirit of God so that the two formed but one flame? What wonders of healing may not one, in whom the ultimate ground of all deigned to manifest itself in a unique way, do? Now Jesus was such a man. Wherever he went power went out of him and healed all who were attuned to the divine, all who had faith. His miracles are therefore instances where nature conformed most to its ultimate law, which is man rooted in God. In them nature was at its most natural because it was at its most human.

Jesus was so taken hold of by the power of God that he could work miracles. We cannot rule out the possibility that even today God so takes hold of the spirit of a man that he becomes capable of healing the souls and bodies of fellowmen by a mere word or gesture. However, such cases can only be exceptional. The exceptional is but a concentrated, intense manifestation of the universal power that every man has in virtue of the original divine command to subdue the earth. This command we fulfill today when we conquer the hostile forces of nature with the help of science and technology.

The fulfillment of this task, by its very nature, devolves primarily on the community and only secondarily on individuals. For only the pooled resources of society as a whole are capable of meeting the magnitude of the challenge posed by natural evils. The working of miracles has therefore become not only a scientific but also an economic and political problem. The command Jesus gave his disciples to work cures and drive out devils thus becomes for us a command to organize our collective resources for the conquest of nature.

But to conquer nature is to humanize it. Man is never fully himself, fully at home in the world, so long as nature is fully the other. He attains to freedom only in the measure in which he refashions nature in his image. He becomes free only in the measure in which he becomes natural, and nature becomes human. Cosmic freedom is the humanization of nature. The liberation of man from nature is, therefore, at the same time the liberation of nature from its nonhuman existence. If so, the New Humanity can come into being only in the New Heaven and the New Earth.

But man's struggle with nature and its forces will lead to authentic freedom only if it has for its aim the well-being of the whole man and of all men. The whole man is man considered in all his dimensions, as body and soul, intelligence and will, action and passion, centred upon himself and centred upon others. Any conquest of nature aimed exclusively at producing material goods to satisfy physical needs can make him only a prisoner of his own needs. To conquer nature for the benefit of the whole man is to produce not only the useful but also the beautiful. Only when the aesthetic becomes its main criterion will production contribute to the wholeness of man. For the aesthetic is a privileged point where the human merges into the divine, where the wholeness of man reflects the wholeness of God.

We said that freedom from cosmic bondage must be won for the whole man and for all men. Deeper reflection will show that this distinction is a false one. For the whole man *is* all men. Every man—in his being, thinking, and loving—includes all men. He must bear the burden of all. The conquest of cosmic forces must, therefore, benefit all men. Hence the perennial relevance of Jesus' compassion for the multitude and of the centrality of love in his teaching. Love as responsibility for one another and for the community must be the beginning and the end, the motive and the final outcome, of all struggle for cosmic freedom.

Where this is not the case every effort at subduing nature serves to fashion ever-new fetters for man. Where the well-being of all is not the determinant form, the fruits of collective research and labour become so many instruments in the hands of the privileged few to inflict hunger, illness, and death on the underprivileged many, as is happening in India. By utilizing natural resources primarily for the production of conspicuous consumption goods, the economic system condemns millions to a subhuman existence which in turn results in illness and premature death. Consider also the danger to life posed by the unhealthy conditions of work in factories, by the proliferation of slums, and by atmospheric pollution. These evils can be obviated only if love finds structural expression in the system of production, distribution, and consumption.

Yet one more condition has to be fulfilled for man's struggle with nature to lead to genuine freedom. Such a struggle has to be guided by the same spirit of God that made it possible for Jesus to work miracles. In other words, it has to be in response to the God who is to come and is already 'becoming' in history. Man should never lose sight of the horizon of the absolute future that beckons him from beyond the beyond. This absolute horizon is not something that limits his possibilities. It is rather the unconditioned condition for the very possibility of transcending all limits. To ignore its call is to run the risk of being imprisoned in one or other of his historically conditioned creations. It is equivalent to the denial of the transcendence of man.

Liberation from cosmic evils, especially from decay and death, is a task that mankind has to accomplish in dialogue with the Lord of history. That this task will be accomplished is a matter of hope. But what of the millions of men and women who came before us only to succumb to the inexorable law of death? What of us who shall not live to see the day when mankind will have brought illness and death under control? To this question we shall return later, in Chapter 9, on existential liberation.

NOTES

1. This knowledge of the common realities permits him to contrast them with the kingdom he is revealing. Cf. Matt. 6:19, 25; 7:27; 11:28; Luke 5:1–11.

2. Sometimes there were nameless crowds: "He saw a great crowd; his heart went out to them, and he cured those who were sick" (Mark 14:14). At other times the occasions are fully described; cf. Mark 1:21–28, 29–31, 40–45; 2:1–12; 3:1–16; 5:25–34; 8:22–26; 9:14–29; Matt. 9:32–34; Luke 13:10–17.

3. Denis E. Nineham, *The Gospel of Saint Mark*, The Pelican Gospel Commentaries (New York: Seabury, 1968; London: Black, 1973), p. 45.

4. See references in note 2 for healings and exorcisms; raisings from the dead: Mark 5:35–43; Luke 7:11–15; John 11:43–44; nature miracles: Mark 6:45–52; 11:12–14; Matt. 17:24–27; Luke 5:1–11; Mark 6:35–41; John 6:1–13; 2:1–11.

5. R. H. Fuller, *Interpreting the Miracles* (London: SCM, 1971; Philadelphia: Westminster, 1963), pp. 24–39.

6. *Ibid.*, p. 41.

V

The Poor Shall Possess the Earth

Man frees himself from the bondage of nature by harnessing its wealth and wresting from it the means whereby he may satisfy his needs. However, in satisfying his basic needs, such as food, clothing, housing, and medicine, he develops ever new and ever more complex needs, which, in their turn, can be satisfied only by still newer forms of struggle with the environment. This process is essentially a social one. Individuals work with and for the community. Where, however, one section of the community has, by some means or other, appropriated the means of production, the rest are condemned to poverty and misery. Thus, in the very struggle to win freedom from cosmic forces, men become the slaves of unjust economic systems.

The Poor of Israel

Economic exploitation and its concomitants, poverty and inequality, have existed in one form or another in all countries ever since the birth of organized social life. And the Palestine of Jesus' time was no exception.[1] There also a wide gulf existed between the rich and the poor. Under the very rich we may mention, first of all, the royal aristocracy of Herod, the imperial aristocracy of the Sadducees who also had their headquarters in the

Holy City, the big absentee landlords who owned large areas of landed property in the countryside, and, finally, the big traders and merchants. There was also a middle class made up of retail traders, and craftsmen owning their own premises.

The bulk of the population belonged to the poorer classes. One such class consisted of the small peasants who cultivated the property of the absentee landlords. They were victims of multiple exploitation, for they were obliged to pay taxes to Rome to the tune of twenty-five percent of the total yield, and tithes to the temple that amounted to twenty-two percent of the remainder. There was also an additional tithe collected to help those among the poor who could not help themselves. Poorer than the small peasants were the wage labourers who were paid one denarius per day, which was scarcely enough for their day-to-day subsistence. Many among them were underemployed or even unemployed. Jesus makes a reference to them in the parable of the workers in the vineyard (Matt. 20:1–7). The small peasants and the workers were at the mercy of the moneylenders. If insolvent, they had no other way out except to sell themselves as slaves to their creditors. The institution of slavery existed in Palestine in the time of Jesus, and there is evidence for it in the Gospels themselves.[2] Slaves, however, did not play any significant role in rural economy, most of them being employed in Jerusalem as domestic servants.

The poor lived in small houses with only one door. Their food consisted of wheat or barley bread and dried fish. They had only one set of clothes each, a tunic and a cloak. Want, insecurity, and misery weighed heavily on their shoulders. How did Jesus respond to their situation? What message had he for the poor and the exploited of his day?

Blessed Are the Poor

The Gospels make it abundantly clear that he considered his mission as principally directed to the poor. "The spirit of the Lord is upon me because he has anointed me; he has sent me to announce good news to the poor" (Luke 4:18). Before proceeding to ascertain the burden of the 'good news' let us examine what he understood by the term *poor*. Did he mean the materially poor or the poor in spirit, i.e., the pious and the humble? The words, cited above, in which he describes his mission, are a free quotation from the prophet Isaiah, ch. 61, where the 'poor' are equated with 'the broken-hearted', 'the captive', 'those in prison', 'those who mourn', and 'the heavy of heart'. This is in itself sufficient indication that the poor stood for people placed in certain objective conditions of misery. This conclusion finds further support in the fact that the Hebrew word for 'poor', *anawim*, literally meant 'bent'. If so, when Isaiah spoke of the poor he had in mind a class of people who were bent under the weight of exploitation and had no one to defend their cause. This meaning accords well with the social conditions in those days, when the rich and the powerful flagrantly violated the rights of the poor.

However, during the subsequent Babylonian exile the word 'poor' took on the additional meaning of 'the pious and the humble', denoting those who looked to God alone for liberation from sorrow and misery. This is understandable enough, since the exiled Jews had lost all their property, and all distinctions between the rich and the poor had vanished. In their total degradation and helplessness they could count on none but God. However, the word 'poor' continued to retain its original reference to a distinct class of people. During the time of Jesus, too, the term had these two dimensions of meaning. We may therefore safely assume that when he spoke of announcing the good news to the poor, he had in mind not only those who cast their hopes on God alone but also the exploited classes, who were materially poor.[3]

The fusion of the two meanings—one economic and the other religious—in the same term 'poor' probably has its social basis in the fact that the materially poor of those days were also the ones who humbly looked to God alone for liberation. The poorer classes had no reason to expect any improvement in their condition either from the geneɪɔsity of the rich or from the initiative of the rulers. Nor could they envisage the possibility of over-throwing the social system through organized revolt. It was therefore natural that they expected God to inter-vene and redress the evil. By and large the same attitude is found even today among the unorganized poor in the villages of India who rely on God or fate to usher in better days.

Let us now come to the more important question: What was the good news Jesus brought to the poor? It was the imminent coming of the reign of God, 'the year of the Lord's favour' (Luke 4:19). Paraphrased, his mes-sage would mean: "The Lord has listened to your cries and lamentations. The time is ripe. The promises made to your fathers are going to be fulfilled. God is soon to come, nay, he is already knocking at your door. He is coming to shatter your fetters and set you free, to satisfy your hunger, to confer on you, the dispossessed, the possession of the earth, and to lead you into the New Heaven and the New Earth"[4] In other words, Jesus an-nounced to the poor and the exploited that God would soon come to vindicate their cause. Nourished as they had been on the Old Testament, his hearers could not have failed to grasp what he meant. They knew that God

was 'the avenger of blood' who never forgets the cry of
the poor (Ps. 9:12), that he lifts the poor man clear of his
troubles (Ps. 107:4), that he richly blesses the destitute
and satisfies the needy with bread (Ps. 132:15), that he
puts the land to rights and shares out afresh its desolate
fields (Isa. 49:8), and that he rescues the poor from those
who do them wrong (Jer. 20:13). They knew too that their
God is no respecter of persons and is not to be bribed,
and that he secures justice for widows and orphans
(Deut. 10:18). They had listened to his words spoken of
old to their forebears: "For crime after crime of Israel I
will grant them no reprieve, because they sell the innocent for silver and the destitute for a pair of shoes. They
grind the heads of the poor into the earth and thrust the
humble out of their way" (Amos 2:6–7). They could not
have forgotten his words spoken through the prophet
Malachi: "I will appear before you in court, prompt to
testify against sorcerers, adulterers, and perjurers,
against those who wrong the hired labourers, the
widow, and the orphan, who thrust the alien aside and
have no fear of me" (Mal. 3:5).

Now *that* God, Jesus told the poor of his day, was soon
to come to set right the wrongs they suffered and to
usher in a new order of things. Did history prove him
right? It didn't. Two thousand years have passed since
he brought the good news. Still the poor are very much
with us. Exploitation and injustice continue to be ram-
pant. The earth is soaked with the blood of the innocent
and the downtrodden. If so, the only conclusion that
would impose itself is that Jesus was mistaken in his
belief that the reign of God was to break out soon. He
erred as many a prophet before him did.

Or, perhaps, we are not fair to him when we say that
he was mistaken. We see error when a statement does
not conform to reality. But every statement has to be

understood against the background of the mental world of the speaker. Now, Jesus' mental world was that of the prophet. As such, he lived in his own time just as a worker lives in his, a lover in his. Time was not for him, as it is for many of us, a long line of which the end is eternity. In his eyes any moment in time was a window opened into that which is beyond time, into eternity understood as fullness of being. In other words, in his prophetic consciousness the eternal impinged on the temporal, the future on the present. The ultimate future and the immediate present coalesced to form but one image. What in reality would require ages for maturation was therefore experienced by him as imminent future, as present, as presenting itself to his senses. We have therefore no right to judge him by our understanding of time. We are closer to the truth when we say that his announcement of the Kingdom was prophetically true, though not historically verified as we understand the term today.

And the prophetic truth which he proclaimed and which is valid for all times may be formulated as follows: 1. God is the absolute, unconditional No to every evil in every form, to everything that destroys the human. 2. As one who rejects evil his coming is always imminent, at every moment irrupting into our lives challenging us to decision. 3. The decision he demands is that we make our own the unconditional No that he is. This last point provides the clue to the riddle why the poor are still with us today. The God of Jesus is a suffering God who cannot fully become what he already is without our lending him a helping hand. Hence the persistent appeals Jesus made to all to decide there and then for God and his kingdom (Matt. 22:1–4; Luke 16:1–13). He called upon them to meet the God who came to meet them and to work with him. But they did fail to respond, just as we have. If, therefore, injustice and oppression continue it is because we have not allowed the divine No to reverberate through our word and deed. It is because we have failed to avenge the blood of the innocent.

From an Economy of Having to an Economy of Giving

As one taken hold of by God, Jesus could not but be the vindicator of the poor. This role he could play all the more effectively because he knew the misery and degradation of the poor from the standpoint of one who belonged to their social condition. Both by circumstances of birth and by choice he was among the poor. He was born into a poor family. This we know from the fact that his mother, Mary, at the time of her purification had to make use of the concession granted to the poor of offering two turtle doves instead of one dove and a lamb (Luke 2:24). His life was of such privation that he could say of himself: "Foxes have their holes, the birds their roosts, but the Son of Man has nowhere to lay his head" (Matt.8:20). On one occasion, when, in the course of a controversy with the lawyers and the Pharisees, he needed a coin to illustrate a point, he had to ask for one from the bystanders, which shows that he did not carry any money with him (Luke 20:24). He lived on charity and had to depend on the help provided by the well-to-do women who accompanied him in his travels (Luke 8:1–3). He looked at poverty with the eyes of the poor. How true was his observation that two copper coins which the poor widow put into the temple treasury meant all she had to live on (Mark 12:41–44). He understood too what trouble a woman takes to find her lost silver piece, and how much she rejoices on finding it again (Luke 15:8–10).

As one among the poor, he must surely have seen the injustices of the prevailing economic system, which allowed a privileged few to grow richer and richer at the expense of the many poor. At the root of such a system lay man's agression against his neighbour. The rich have their hands dripping with the blood of the poor and the exploited. Besides, they set up riches as the supreme object of worship and thereby cease to be worshippers of the true God. "No servant can be the slave of two masters; for either he will hate the first and love the second, or he will be devoted to the first and think nothing of the second. You cannot serve God and money" (Matt. 6:24). That is why Jesus said: "How hard it will be for the wealthy to enter the kingdom of God! . . . It is easier for a camel to pass through the eye of a needle than for a rich man to enter the kingdom of God" (Mark 10:23–25). It is an illusion for the rich to think that they can belong to the kingdom while remaining within the economic system that made them rich. This is, in fact, the burden of the story of the rich young man who came to Jesus with the question: "Good Teacher, what must I do to inherit eternal life?" (Mark 10:17). On being told that he should observe all the commandments, his answer was: "But Master, I have kept all these since I was a boy." Which shows that he was one who strictly observed the Law, but within the system of private owership. Jesus, however, demanded something more: "One thing you lack: go, sell everything you have, and *give* to the poor, and you will have riches in heaven; and come, follow me." Paradoxically, what the man lacked had something to do with what he had in plenty, namely, riches. How could he inherit eternal life so long as he clung to an economic system which violently deprived the many of their inheritance of the earth? To become a member of the community of the future he had to sell what he had and give to the poor. In other words, he had to break with the economy of private property and embrace an economy of giving. This he was not prepared to do. Hence his departure with a sad face.

The Poor Shall Possess the Earth

Contrasted with him, the disciples of Jesus were prepared to rupture the bonds of private property. Simon and Andrew "left their nets and followed him" (Mark 1:18). The sons of Zebedee went off to follow him "leaving their father Zebedee in the boat with the hired men" (Mark 1:20). Similarly, Levi, the tax-collector, relinquished his lucrative job and followed Jesus empty-handed. The other disciples did the same, as is clear from Peter's claim: "We here have left everything to become your followers" (Mark 1:28). What they did at the outset of their discipleship was to determine also their subsequent mission to preach the good news, work cures, and drive out demons. They were instructed not to rely on private property in the form of bread, bag, money, or even an extra tunic, but to live from hospitality; i.e., from an economy of giving (Mark 6:7–13). When he was faced with a large famished crowd, Jesus rejected the disciples' suggestion that they buy provisions from the villages near by. Instead he asked them to give what they had, being sure that what was given in love would multiply and meet the needs of all (Mark 6:34–44).[6] That he also taught his disciples to devalue the money economy seems to be implied in his comment on the widow's mite: "I tell you this, this poor widow has given more than any of the others; for those others who have given had more than enough, but she, with less than enough, has given all that she had to live on" (Mark 12:43–44). Here too we meet with a paradox. She who gave least gave most. What mattered in the eyes of Jesus was not the exchange-value of what she put in (which was but little) but its use-value (which was much, being all that she had to live on).[7]

It follows from our analysis that the life and message of Jesus was in principle disruptive of the prevailing economic system. However, for him criticism of the existing conditions was but a prerequisite for marching ahead to a new order of things. Consequently the demand: "Follow me." And the guiding principle of the new social order to which his followers were to commit themselves is well expressed in his saying: "Take note of what you hear; the measure you *give* is the measure you will receive, with something more besides." (Mark 4:24). The 'something more besides' which he promised represents the fullness of the age to come, a fullness which is to be understood also in the material sense. In an economic order in which each gives what he has, each also receives thewhole of what the community has. Here lies the secret of the superabundance that will characterize the community of the future. In order to express the plenty that will mark the new age, Jesus uses many and varied symbols: the seed buried in the ground which produces first the blade, then the ear, the *full grain* in the ear (Mark 4:28); the mustard seed that becomes the *greatest* of all shrubs (Mark 4:32); the seed that fell into the good soil and grew up yielding thirtyfold and sixtyfold and a *hundredfold* (Mark 4:1–9); and the few loaves which, multiplied, *satisfied all* (Mark 6:42 and 8:8). The disciples who left everything to follow him receive the promise of plenty in terms of material goods and social fellowship. "I tell you this: there is no one who has given up home, brothers or sisters, mother, father or children, or land, for my sake and for the Gospel, who will not receive in this age *a hundred times as much*—houses, brothers and sisters, mothers and children, and land—and persecution besides; and in the age to come eternal life"

(Mark 10:29–30. It is disputed whether or not this phrase 'and in the age to come eternal life' is part of the authentic saying of Jesus.[8] Even if it were, it could not have meant a spiritual world above this world of ours, because such a concept was alien to the Hebrew mode of thinking. The essential thing to remember is that the fullness of the age to come is at once continuous and discontinuous with the present age: continuous, because it is our earth (land, houses) and our society (mothers, brothers, sisters) filled with an abiding love; discontinuous, because it is the *definitive* superseding of all alienation.

The earliest community of believers understood very well the call of their master to relinquish the economy of private property and commit themselves to an economy of giving which multiplies the given and satisfies the needs of all. Their practice is, in fact, the best commentary on that future that Jesus envisioned. "The whole body of believers was united in heart and soul. Not a man of them claimed any of his possessions as his own, but everything was held in common, while the apostles bore witness with great power to the resurrection of the Lord Jesus. They were all held in high esteem; for they had never a needy person among them, because all who had property in land or houses sold it, brought the proceeds of the sale, and laid the money at the feet of the apostles; it was then distributed to any who stood in need" (Acts 4:32–35). From each according to his ability, to each according to his need—such was the economic creed of the earliest community of disciples.

All four Gospels testify to Jesus's profound concern for the poor and to his stringent criticism of the rich. This should not, however, be interpreted to mean that in his view the rich are necessarily barred from entering the kingdom of God or that poverty in itself assures entry into it. The rich have access to the New Age provided they are prepared to call in question the conditions that have made them rich and to give up their possessions in response to the call of the Kingdom. The rich young man forfeited his chance to enter the Kingdom when he refused to part with his wealth, whereas Zacchaeus, although rich, met his salvation because he showed himself willing to put an end to his exploitations of the people and give away half his possessions in charity (Luke 19:8–10).The poor also, no less than the rich, have to put the reign of God before everything else. Mere material poverty is no passport for entry into the New Humanity. Just as the rich can make an idol of the riches they already have, so can the poor, the riches they long to have. However, such a warning was not necessary for the poor of Jesus' time, since they, expecting little from their own initiative or from an initiative on the part of guardians of the status quo, looked to God alone for liberation. It is this openness to the future, not their passive acceptance of their lot, which is to be regarded as of permanent value in their attitude. For how can the poor of any age be fit for an economy of giving if they cling to the relics of the past or the realities of the present? No radical change, personal or social, is possible so long as the enslaved love their own fetters. The kingdom of God will belong to the poor only if they are also poor in spirit; i.e., open to the future. The openness in question must manifest itself as a hungering and thirsting for justice, as an organized struggle for liberation, even to the point of inviting repression from the powers that be. "Blessed are those who are presecuted for the cause of justice, for theirs is the kingdom of heaven" (Matt. 5: 10).

NOTES

1. On this point see Joachim Jeremias, *Jerusalem in the Time of Jesus* (London: SCM, and Philadelphia: Fortress, 1969), Ch. 6.

2. Modern versions use *servant* rather than *slave* for *doulos* in such texts as Matt. 24:45–51; Luke 12:42–48; and 17:7–10. A domestic slave could become manager or steward.

3. Jeremias, NTT, pp. 112–13.

4. Cf. the Beatitudes, Matt. 5:3–10, and the Isaiahan text that Jesus applies to himself, Luke 4:18–21.

5. See Fernando Belo, *Lecture materialiste de l'Evangile de Marc* (Paris: Cerf, 1975), pp. 233–37.

VI

Towards the Total Man

The Despised of the Earth

Man cannot live on bread alone; he lives also on every word uttered by his fellowmen whereby he is recognized as a person and accepted as an equal. If some are poor and destitute it is because others have refused to recognize them as brothers and equals. The wealth of the few is achieved at the cost of the want of many. Only those can amass wealth who choose to reduce their fellowmen to the condition of mere objects which they can manipulate at will. Economic inequality, therefore, carries with it social inequality. Poverty has for its concomitant social degradation. The poor are also the unloved and the unwanted of the earth.

This was true also of the poor of Jesus' day. But in their case poverty bore an additional social stigma insofar as it was considered a sign of divine punishment, just as wealth was attributed to divine favour. However, poverty did not necessarily imply social degradation; nor did wealth necessarily win popular esteem. For instance the publicans, though wealthy, were held in contempt, whereas such doctors of the law as happened to be poor were nevertheless esteemed.

There were also other factors on the basis of which large sections of the population were either despised or even rendered social outcasts.[1] One such factor was occupational taboo. Those who engaged in certain professions were deprived of civil and political rights, besides being despised and hated by the people. Such, for instance, were gamblers with dice, usurers, pigeon-trainers, dealers in the produce of the Sabbatical year, herdsmen, tax collectors, and publicans. They were hated for indulging in swindling or resorting to extortion. There were others, such as goldsmiths, flaxcombers, handmill cleaners, weavers, barbers, and launderers, who incurred social opprobrium for the, to us, curious reason that they had to deal with women in plying their trade and, for that reason, were morally suspect. To the socially disreputable belonged also slaves and the racially impure, such as bastards, the fatherless, foundlings, eunuchs, and the illegitimate descendants of proselytes. If even those with only slight racial blemish were the object of orthodox scorn, how much more the gentiles! The latter were in fact considered outside the pale of divine favour.

Though not despised, the womenfolk occupied an inferior position in Jewish society. Their condition finds a fairly accurate description in the saying of Josephus: "A woman is in every respect of less worth than a man."[2] Even in religious matters women were considered inferior to men. In the temple they had access only to the court set apart for them. They were exempted from reciting the shema morning and evening, because, like slaves, they had no right to dispose of their time. Those belonging to the higher social circles in the cities had to confine themselves within their houses. Men considered it a virtue not to have any social contact with them. A rabbinic proverb ran: "Do not speak much with womankind."[3] In the countryside, however, especially among the poorer classes the women folk enjoyed greater freedom.

Far removed from the despised classes and comfortably anchored in their own self-righteousness stood the respectable classes—the Pharisees, the scribes, the priests and, generally, the rich. They avoided any contact with the socially underprivileged lest they be defiled. It was into such a society fragmented by false religion and morality that Jesus came. How did he react to it? Both his teaching and conduct constituted a defiance of the status quo and a declaration of solidarity with the outcasts of society.

The Dream of the Total Man

The despised classes received the good news from Jesus, that the final coming of God will coincide with the 'becoming' of mankind into his people, into a community bound by love, that he will gather together and weld the many fragments of humanity into the Total Man. The birth of the Total Man will result in liberation from all social barriers, and from inequality, injustice, and oppression. Naturally Jesus did not give expression to this hope in conceptual language. Instead he used symbols and images drawn from the religious heritage of his people.

He speaks of the New Humanity as the flock which he gathers around him and for which he gives his life (Luke 12:32; John 10:14–15). He refers to it as the family of God (Matt. 23:8–9), as the banquet of salvation (Matt. 8:11), as God's plantation (Matt. 13:24 ff.), as a net that a fisherman casts into the sea to gather in fishes of all sorts (Matt. 13:47 ff.) as the temple of God (Mark 14:58), as the assembly of God (Matt. 16:18 ff.), and as the people of the New Covenant (Matt. 26:28). All these symbols stress one thing: What Jesus envisions is the salvation not of the individual in isolation but of the community of men. The ultimate possibilities of man can be realized only in a

people centred upon God. So too in a community can
God become what he already is.

Does this mean that for Jesus what mattered was the
collectivity and not the individual? Does this mean that
he subordinated the individual to the community as a
means to an end? Not at all. For him the collective was
not an abstraction but a communion of persons bound by
love. For this very reason he was also concerned with the
final liberation of the individual. There are many sayings
and parables that testify to this. Inclusion in the New
Humanity is conditional upon the personal decision of
each (Mark 3:31–35). The God of Jesus is like a shepherd
who leaves the ninety-nine in the open pasture and goes
after the missing one until he has found it (Luke 15:3–6).
He is one who cares for the least and the last: "Anything
you did for one of my brothers here, however humble,
you did for me" (Matt.25:40). Hence Jesus' vision of the
Total Man steers clear of both collectivism, which con-
siders the individual merely as a function of the group,
and individualism, which subordinates the group to the
individual and his private salvation.

The New Humanity is the definitive supersession of all
barriers consisting of exclusive claims and privileges. It is
constituted on the basis of neither kinship, nor religion,
nor race. Once, while addressing a crowd, word was
brought to him that his mother and brothers were standing outside asking for him. He replied: "Who is my
mother? Who are my brothers?" And pointing to those
who were sitting around and listening to him, he said:
"Here are my mother and my brothers. Whoever does
the will of God is my brother, my sister, my mother"
(Mark 3:31–35). What is envisioned here is a new community that transcends all bounds set by kinship, one
whose sole principle of unity consists in doing the will of
God. Neither is entry into the New Humanity deter-

mined by membership in any particular race or religious
community. This is borne out by the fact that Jesus pro-
poses a Samaritan as the model of behaviour proper to
the New Age. The latter is commended simply because
he responded to one in need of help. The helper's race or
religion was immaterial.

The truth that the New Humanity is open to all irrespective of racial or cultural distinctions comes out
clearly in the cleansing of the temple, which is a parable
in action. The key to its proper understanding are the
words: "Does not the Scripture say, 'My house shall be
called a house of prayer *for all the nations*'? But you have
made it a robbers' cave" (Mark 11:17). That the temple
was destined for worship by all nations was indicated by
the fact that a section of it was set apart for the use of the
gentiles. It was precisely there, in the 'court of the gentiles', that Jesus saw trafficking going on. Therefore, by
upsetting the tables of moneychangers and the seats of
dealers in pigeons, he was doing nothing less than vin-
dicating the rights of the gentiles to offer worship to
God. Before God there is no distinction between Jew or
gentile. This idea is expressed much more forcefully in
the saying of Jesus that the temple itself will be destroyed
to make way for another one not made with human
hands (Mark 14:58). The new temple is the new community of men which God will gather around him to
offer worship 'in spirit and in truth' (John 4:23).

He found faith, which is the condition for belonging to
the New Age, also among non-Jews like the Samaritan
leper (Luke 17:11–19), the Syrophoenician woman (Mark
7:26–30), and the gentile nobleman. It was of the last-
mentioned Jesus said: "I tell you, nowhere, not even in
Israel, have I found faith like this" (Luke 7: 10). Gentiles
were also recipients of the favours of the New Age, as is
clear from the miracles worked in their behalf. The all-

inclusiveness of the reign of God will find its final expression at the summing up of history when "many will
come from east and west to feast with Abraham, Isaac,
and Jacob in the kingdom of Heaven" (Matt. 8:11).

The Social Practice of Jesus

It is in the light of this hope for the New Age that Jesus
lived and moved among men. It also determined his
attitude towards the outcasts of society. As a prophet
and a teacher he was expected to associate himself exclusively with the respectable classes. In reality it was,
above all, the despised and the disreputable he chose to
mingle with. He saw in them the stuff out of which the
New Humanity will be formed. For only they, in his
view, were open to all the possibilities of man, and
disposed to welcome the initiatives of God. That is why
he said to the respectable classes who prided themselves
upon being the favoured friends of God: "I tell you this:
tax-gatherers and prostitutes are entering the kingdom
of God ahead of you." In Aramaic, the language Jesus
spoke, the statement would have meant: "I tell you this:
tax-gatherers and prostitutes will enter the kingdom of
God, and *not you*" (Matt. 21:31).[4] One can well imagine
how shocking these words would have been to the orthodox Jews who gloried in their self-righteousness. The
offense was carried still further when Jesus invited the
outcasts of society to sit at table with him. "When Jesus
was at table in his house, many bad characters
—tax-gatherers and others—were seated with him and
his disciples; for there were many who followed him.
Some doctors of the law who were Pharisees noticed him
eating in this bad company, and said to his disciples, 'He
eats with tax-gathers and sinners!' Jesus heard it and said
to them, 'It is not the healthy that need a doctor, but the
sick; I did not come to invite virtuous people, but sin-

ners' " (Mark 2:15–17). Now eating for the Jews, was something more than merely satisfying a bodily need. More importantly, it was a form of social intimacy. When, therefore, Jesus invited social outcasts to sit at the table with him he was in fact offering them intimate human fellowship. What is more, the fellowship he offered was in the real sense also divine. Among the Jews, common meals had a religious significance. Food and drink shared was a symbol of fellowship with God. By eating and drinking with the socially despised, Jesus showed in deed that God was with them as one who accepted them as they were and came to meet their need. For they were like the sick who needed the services of a doctor and knew that they needed it. True, the respectable people too were objectively in need of God, but in their pride did not recognize it and thereby shut him out from their lives.

No wonder the teachings and practice of the young rabbi from Nazareth profoundly shocked the religious sensibilities of the orthodox Jewry. Hence their mocking description of him as a 'glutton and a drunkard, a friend of publicans and sinners' (Matt. 11:19).By his conduct he repudiated all the artificial barriers that false religion and morality had set up between man and man. What he did was a powerful onslaught on the walls erected by the privileged classes between God and the unfortunate among his children. It challenged the religious arrogance of the orthodox Jews who looked upon God as their monopoly and used him to safeguard their vested interests. Positively, the practice of commensal fellowship with social outcasts meant for Jesus a partial anticipation of the New Humanity in which all the children of God will gather around to sit at table with him in total love and self-giving.

The practice of table-fellowship occupied a central position in the life of Jesus. It summed up in deed the whole of his preaching. It was therefore but natural that on the eve of that fateful day when he knew that he was going to be killed, he, as usual, invited such of his friends as were with him to share his meal for the last time. The so-called Last Supper is but the culmination of the innumerable suppers he had had with his disciples and with all those who sincerely sought the face of God. It is in these frequent meals that we have to seek the deeper roots of what subsequently came to be called the Eucharist.[5]

Originally the Eucharist was a full meal like any family meal in a Jewish home. It was only later that the emphasis shifted from the meal as a whole to two of its elements, namely, the bread and the wine, symbols respectively of the body and blood of Jesus.[6] Naturally the body and blood in question could only be those of the risen Jesus, who is outside the flux of history. This meant a twofold alienation. First, the symbolism of the meal was impoverished. Second, the prophetic meaning of the Eucharist as the anticipation, in symbol as well as in reality, of the New Humanity of the end-time was lost sight of. This makes it all the more necessary for us to go back to the table-fellowship of Jesus and from its vantage point recapture the original meaning of the Eucharist.

Reinterpreted in the light of the meals Jesus used to have with social and religious outcasts, the words attributed to Jesus, 'This is my body, this is my blood' may be paraphrased thus: "When you come together in the name of your common hope in the New Humanity without distinction of classes and, in love, share the fruits of your labour, you are truly making your own my faith, my hope, my commitment, and my destiny. Thereby you become in the real sense my flesh and blood, my prolongation in history." It is only when the products of labour like food and drink become the bond between man and man instead of being instruments of exploitation of man by man, it is only when the world of things mediates man's love for God and his fellowmen, that the meaning of Jesus' table-fellowship becomes realized in history. Seen in this perspective, the love-meal Jesus instituted is an invitation to overthrow all structures of inequality and to construct a new social order in which every man is his brother's keeper.

The same fundamental option that moved him to seek the company of the marginalized also determined his choice of disciples. These too belonged to the despised classes. He spoke of them as 'the little ones' (Mark 9:42), 'the humble' (Matt. 25:40), 'the simple' as opposed to the wise, and the uneducated, the ignorant, in short, of those for whom, according to prevailing conceptions, salvation was difficult, if not impossible. The historical movement he initiated was, in the main, of the lowest stratum of Jewish society. In no sense of the term was it elitist.

No less revolutionary than Jesus' table-fellowship with publicans and sinners was his rejection of the social taboos surrounding relations between the sexes. Nothing, perhaps, was more shocking for his contemporaries than the freedom with which he associated himself with women, considering the inferior position of women in Jewish society. Though a bachelor, he had close friends among them, as is clear from the story of Martha and Mary (Luke 10:38–42). We find a retinue of women accompanying him wherever he went and supporting him out of their own means (Mark 15:40–41; Luke 8:1–3). He allowed a woman of doubtful reputation to wash his feet with her tears and wipe them with her hair (Luke 7:37–38). Contrary to the accepted social norms he freely engaged in conversation with a woman he met casually by a well-side, something that amazed even his disciples

(John 4:27). He also worked miracles in their favour (Luke 8:43; 7:11–15). Not only men but also women were to be found among his audience (Luke 11:27).

In accord with his conduct was also his teaching on marriage. He annulled the prevailing custom, which permitted a man to discharge his wife on any silly pretext merely by giving her a bill of divorce, and, thereby, he restored the indissolubility of marriage as originally willed by the Creator (Mark 10:2–9). By enjoining also on the woman the obligation not to initiate proceedings of divorce against her husband, he implicitly affirmed the fundamental equality of man and woman as persons (Mark 10:11–12). The same equality finds expression in his saying: "Whoever does the will of God is my brother, my sister, my mother" (Mark 3:35). Here the value of a person is judged solely by the standard of obedience to the will of God and not by that of the distinction of sexes.

All this means that with Jesus a new spirit entered into history, a spirit that could not be contained within the wineskins of the old social and religious traditions, and was bound to burst them from within. It was a spirit of refusal and acceptance: refusal of every mutilation and fragmentation of man, and acceptance of togetherness in love and mutual concern as authentic human existence. This new social ethos did in fact give history a new orientation by shattering old fetters and creating new bonds between men. But in the course of time its destructive-constructive force came to be domesticated, if not smothered, by the same community whose mission it was to keep it alive and active. Now the time has come to release its pristine energies for the construction of a new humanity.

NOTES

1. Joachim Jeremias, *Jerusalem in the Time of Jesus* (London: SCM, and Philadelphia: Fortress, 1969), Ch. 14 to 18.

2. Jeremias, NTT, p. 266.

3. *Ibid.*, (For a fuller discussion on the position of women in Jewish society, see his *Jerusalem in the Time of Jesus,* Ch. 18.

4. See Jeremias, NTT, p. 117.

5. *Ibid.,* pp. 289–90.

6. Willi Marxen, "The Lord's Supper: Concepts and Developments," in *Jesus in His Time,* ed. Hans Jürgen Schultz (London: SPCK, and Philadelphia: Fortress, 1971), pp. 106–14.

VII

The Cost of Freedom:
Political Death

Of all the sufferings of the Jewish people the most intensely felt was their subjection to Roman domination.
Jesus himself could not have been unaware of it, coming
as he did from Galilee, whose inhabitants were known
for their fanatical zeal for the ancient traditions and for
their struggle against foreign powers. Conscious of his
mission to set free the oppressed, he could not have
avoided taking a stand with regard to Rome either. What
was that stand? Before attempting an answer let us focus
clearly the historical setting.

The Challenge of Foreign Domination

After their return from the Babylonian exile (586–538
B.C.) the Jews had settled down in their native land,
secure in the hope of a long period of peace and prosper-
ity to come. But their hopes never fructified. They were
destined to live as a subject people under successive
foreign powers—the Persians, the Greeks, the Egyptians, the Syrian Seleucids, the Parthians and, finally,
the Romans. Palestine came under Roman power in 63
B.C. when Pompey conquered Jerusalem. The Romans
appointed Herod, a half-Jewish Idumean, as the king of

the Jews. On his death in 4 B.C. the kingdom was divided among his sons by Emperor Augustus. Archelaus ruled Judea in the south, while Herod Antipas ruled Galilee. The former was, however, deposed in 6 A.D. for reasons of misrule, and his territory passed into the direct charge of the Romans. But as far as the common man was concerned, the rule of Herod was as detestable as that of the Romans.

The people had ample reasons to feel resentment against Rome. The Law had forbidden setting up a foreigner to rule over them; Yahweh alone was to be their king (Deut. 17:15). The Roman practice of census, too, met with popular disapproval, since Yahweh had censured David for numbering his subjects (2 Sam 24). Worse still, the Roman procurator, Pilate, had only contempt for the natives, and went out of his way to humiliate them. He revoked the order, which his predecessors had passed as a concession to Jewish religious sensibilities, that the Roman army should remove the Emperor's image from its standards whenever it entered the Holy City. He even looted the temple treasury, a deed deemed sacrilegious by every Jew. The reference in Luke 13:2 to the many Galileans who were slaughtered by Pilate while they were offering worship in the temple, is further proof of his ruthless character. No less unwelcome to the people were the economic consequences of Roman rule. The burden of taxation weighed heavily on them and it was further aggravated by the unscrupulous manner in which the tax-gatherers went about their business. In the prevailing circumstances only those who collaborated with the foreign regime could succeed in getting rich. Did all these grievances lead to a popular revolt?

There was in fact a tradition of popular resistance to foreign domination. When in 168 B.C. the Syrian king,

Antiochus Epiphanes, conquered Jerusalem, desecrated the temple, and tried to destroy Jewish religion by introducing Hellenistic cults, the people rose to a man in revolt under the leadership of the Maccabees and threw out the hated aliens. Again in 6 A.D. when the Romans introduced taxation, a certain Judas of Galilee raised a rebellion which, however, was ruthlessly put down by Quirinus, the governor of Syria. Though the revolt was a failure, it gave birth to an extremist movement whose members were called the Zealots. The word *zealot* meant those who were prepared even to use force in defence of the traditional law, which, as we have seen, forbade rule by foreigners. It is not certain whether Zealotism already existed as a political party in the time of Jesus. Probably it was then no more than an underground movement indulging in sporadic acts of violence.[1] However that may be, we find a representative of this radical wing among the disciples of Jesus.

However, not all Jews were committed to driving out the Romans by force. The religious power structure was dominated by the Sadducees,[2] who formed an aristocracy of about two hundred families. It is from among them that the High Priests were drawn. Unlike the Essenes and the Pharisees, the Sadducees constituted a political party. They made up the hard core of the Sanhedrin, the High Court of Justice. They enjoyed controlled autonomy in the internal matters of Jewish society. For the rest they were mere puppets in the hands of Rome. They had everything to gain by following a pacifist policy in political matters. First, there was the perennial lure of power itself, religious as well as political. Besides, in charge of the temple, the priestly ruling class controlled the treasury and, at the time of great festivals, carried on a lucrative business in foreign exchange.

The other dominant group, the Pharisees, too, followed a policy of pacifism vis-à-vis the occupying power. They were professedly religious men and did not concern themselves with politics except when their religious sensibilities were outraged. When in 6 B.C. Herod put up a golden eagle over the main entrance of the temple, they struck it down, for which some among them had to pay the penalty of being burned alive. In normal times, however, they held to the view that God was making use of Rome to chastise Israel for its infidelities and sins.

No to Political Messianism

Any consideration of Jesus' political attitudes has to start with the undeniable fact that he was put to death by crucifixion by the then Roman procurator, Pontius Pilate. Crucifixion was a Roman penalty, which implies that the authorities conducted a formal trial and found the accused guilty. What then was the accusation? The charge sheet affixed to the cross read, 'Jesus of Nazareth, king of the Jews.' This means that Jesus was accused of leading a rebellion against Rome with the intention of installing himself as king. This is borne out also by the charge the Jewish leaders brought against him before the Roman tribunal. "We found this man subverting our nation, opposing the payment of taxes to Caesar, and claiming to be Messiah, a king" (Luke 23:2). Was this accusation true? When asked by Pilate, "Are you the king of the Jews?" Jesus gave what sounds like an evasive answer: "The words are yours" (Mark 15:2). His reply has been variously interpreted—as affirmative, as negative, or as noncommittal. One thing is certain. He could not have admitted to being king of the Jews in the sense of a political Messiah. To grasp this we have to interpret Jesus' words in the context of his life and teaching as a whole.

Right at the beginning of his public career the Spirit of God invaded him and drove him into the desert, there to be tempted by Satan. What the Gospels describe as three distinct temptations are but variations of one temptation, namely, to follow the way of the political messianism.[3] "Again, the devil took him to a very high mountain, and showed him all the kingdoms of the world and the glory of them; and he said to him, 'All these I will give you, if you will fall down and worship me' " (Matt. 4:8–10). What Satan held up before Jesus was the Zealot ideal of an Israel ruling over all the kingdoms of the world. But that ideal was against the original revelation from God which forbade Israel to have anyone but God to rule over them. Hence Jesus' reply: "Begone, Satan! for it is written, 'You shall worship the Lord your God and him only shall you serve' " (Matt. 4:10).It is against this background that we should understand his other saying: "For what does it profit a man, to gain the whole world and forfeit his life?" (Mark 8:36). What use gaining universal political power if thereby man is denied the possibility of leading a rich and full life?

In the desert Jesus definitively opted against political messianism. And Satan retreated for the time being, but only to reappear and confront him with the same temptation at various points in his life. He did so first through the people, who by and large shared the Zealot hopes. There are indications in the Gospels that the crowd, on seeing the marvels he worked, began to nurse the hope that he would come out into the open and proclaim himself the political leader they were eagerly awaiting. This explains their persistent efforts to pursue him wherever he went. Equally persistently he withdrew from them. We find him seeking clandestinity in private homes (Mark 1:29; 3:1; 3:19; 7:24), in desert places (Mark 1:35; 6:31), by the seaside (Mark 2:13; 3:7; 4:1), and in boats (Mark 4:35; 5:21; 6:45; 8:10, 13). The Gospel according to John explicitly states that when, after the miraculous feeding of the multitude, Jesus realized that the people wanted to seize him and proclaim him a king, he "withdrew again to the hills by himself" (John 6:14–15). The contrast between the nationalist hopes of the people and the role he assigned to himself may be seen also in the narrative of his entry into Jerusalem. The crowd acclaimed him with the words: "Hosanna! Blessed is he who comes in the name of the Lord! Blessed is the kingdom of our father David that is coming! Hosanna in the highest!" (Mark 11: 9–10). This shows that they expected him to restore the kingdom of David. This conclusion imposes itself all the more if 'Hosanna in the highest' meant, as a recent interpreter has tried to show. 'Save us from the Romans'.[5] That any such plan was foreign to the mind of Jesus follows from the fact that he chose for his means of transportation a colt rather than a horse, the beast of war par excellence.

Yet on another occasion did Satan raise his head, this time in the person of Peter. When, at Caesarea Philippi, Jesus asked his disciples what they thought of him, Peter enthusiastically replied "You are the Messiah." But what he meant by that term was a political Messiah who would rule over the nations. This is clear from the sequel of the story. For, when Jesus went on to say that his destiny was to go to Jerusalem, there to face death at the hands of his enemies, Peter took him by the arm and began to rebuke him saying: "Heaven forbid! . . . No, Lord, this shall never happen to you." At this he got the stunning reply: "Away with you, Satan. You think as men think, not as God thinks" (Mark 8:27–33). Nor were the thoughts of the other disciples any less the thoughts of men, as may be seen from their quarrel as to who should be greatest in the kingdom of God (Mark 9:33–34), from the request of the sons of Zebedee to be allowed to sit one on his right and the other on his left when he came in glory (Mark 10:37), and from the fact that one of the disciples betrayed him, and another resorted to violence and struck off the ear of the High Priest's servant.

Seen in the light of his resolute opposition to political messianism, the agony in the Garden of Olives assumes special significance. It looks as though the ideological rift between himself, on the one hand, and the disciples and the crowd, on the other, took on, on the eve of his death, the form of a chasm in his own soul between what he willed (the thoughts of men) and what God willed (the thoughts of God): "Abba, Father, all things are possible to thee; remove this cup from me; yet not *what I will*, but what thou wilt" (Mark 14:36).[6] The agony ends with his final acceptance of the thoughts and purposes of God. With that decisive victory won, he surrendered himself to his enemies.

His teaching too was in accord with his repudiation of the Zealot ideal of a restored theocracy. We do not find in it overtones of Jewish nationalism, as would have been the case if he were committed to political messianism. Besides, he did what no Zealot would ever have dreamt of doing: he foretold the destruction of the temple, the very centre and hearth of Jewish religion (Mark 13:2). Relevant in this context is also his teaching on nonviolence. A person who required of his disciples that, if anyone should slap them on their right cheek, they should turn and offer him their left as well, could never have been a follower of the Zealots, who indulged in violence (Matt. 5:39).

The Cost of Freedom: Death on the Cross

It follows from our discussion thus far that Jesus' response before Pilate could not have meant an admission of his being the messianic king of the Jews. Does this mean that he was indifferent to the political slavery of his people or that he was a political conformist? On the contrary. His very commitment to the Kingdom as a community of freedom brought him into conflict with the political power not only of Rome but also of the Sanhedrin in Jerusalem and of Herod in Galilee.

Herod, whose territory was the main scene of Jesus' activity, had John the Baptizer beheaded for criticizing his incestuous relationship with his brother's wife (Mark 6: 14–29). By censuring the immoral conduct of the king, John implicitly questioned the divine legitimization of his authority to rule. If so, Herod had equal reason to get rid of Jesus as well, for he too preached the indissolubility of marriage, all the more so since he believed the latter to be John himself risen from the dead. Luke, in fact, explicitly states that some Pharisees approached Jesus in order to persuade him to quit Galilee because Herod was seeking to kill him (Luke 13:31). That Jesus himself was aware of the threat may be seen from his reply to them: "Go and tell that fox, 'Behold, I cast out demons and perform cures today and tomorrow, and the third day I finish my course' " (Luke 13:32).

Jesus' teaching and conduct was subversive also of the religious-political power of the Sanhedrin. First, his radical interpretation of the Law, his rejection of the distinction between the sacred and the profane, his re-affirmation of the primacy of love over cult, and his prediction of the destruction of the temple, undermined the religious authority of the High Priesthood. Second, the universal character of the New Humanity that he proclaimed contradicted the nationalist particularism of the Jewish authorities. Third, the ruling clique had a vested interest in maintaining the status quo, since they ruled by the favour of Rome. And it was just the status quo of their use of religious political power to exploit the people that Jesus challenged when he threw out the vendors and the money-changers from the temple. Hence their question: "By what authority are you acting like this?" (Mark 11:28). In all likelihood the cleansing of the temple was the immediate provocation that led to Jesus' arrest and trial before the Sanhedrin.

Now we come to the crucial question: Did Jesus oppose Roman imperialism in Palestine? Much as he rejected the reformist, nationalist aspirations of the Zealots, he certainly shared their opposition to foreign domination. Very much to the point is the well-known saying of his: "Render to Caesar the things that are Caesar's, and to God the things that are God's" (Mark 12:17).[7] At first blush his reply sounds like an advice to abide by the Roman laws of taxation. But we must remember that it was to trap him in words that the Pharisees and the followers of Herod came up with the question whether it was lawful to pay taxes to Rome. If he said yes, he would thereby have declared himself a friend of the Romans and an enemy of the people. If, on the contrary, he said no, he could have been produced before the Roman authorities on the charge of sedition. His answer therefore had necessarily to be guarded, which makes it equally necessary for us to read between the lines. To arrive at the true meaning we have to keep in mind the creation story in Genesis according to which man alone was made in God's image, and, further, the Jewish belief that Israel was forbidden by God to make images of anything in heaven or on earth (Deut. 5:8). To use coins bearing the image of Caesar was therefore contrary to the will of God. Hence 'Render to Caesar the things that are Caesar's' could as well have meant: "Have nothing to do with this coin or with the economic and political power it represents. Return it to Caesar whose image it bears. But you, unlike this coin, bear the image of God and, as such, belong to him. To him alone therefore shall you be subject, to no one else, not even to Caesar." Naturally, this meaning could have been grasped only by those 'who had ears to hear', i.e. by those whose hearts were not hardened by the worship of idols.

A more explicit and unambiguous rejection of foreign domination is contained in the words: "You know that in the world the recognized rulers lord it over their subjects and make them feel the weight of authority. That is not the way with you; among you, whoever wants to be great must be your servant, and whoever wants to be first must be the willing slave of all" (Mark 10:42–45). Here the subversiveness of Jesus' teaching extends beyond the Jewish and the Roman power structures to all states that use their authority to grind the heads of people in the mud.

In yet another sense did Jesus pose a threat to Roman imperialism. The Romans needed the support of the Sanhedrin to maintain their rule in Palestine, which the latter was all too willing to provide. And it was just this support that Jesus threatened to weaken, if not to destroy, when he used his prophetic authority to cleanse the temple and preached a message that shook the religious foundations of the priestly ruling class. Such being the case, it was in the interests of Pilate as well as to get rid of the prophet from Galilee.

This brings us to the crucial truth often forgotten by the followers of Jesus. Traditional teaching has instilled in them the idea that Jesus' death is, as it were, a thing apart, in itself endowed with value as sacrifice offered to God, as if it had no relation to his teaching and practice. The truth is that his life was prematurely and brutally brought to an end by the collusion of the religious and political powers of his day who found in his life and teaching a threat to their own survival. Death was the price he had to pay for his merciless criticism of religious formalism and bigotry, for his condemnation of the religious authorities who sought to cleverly combine the service of God with the service of Mammon, for his fellowship with the outcasts of society, for his commitment to a New Humanity open to all who hunger and thirst for justice, in one word, for his having sought first and above all things the kingdom of God and its justice. And he opted to pay the price, knowing full well what it would cost him in terms of human suffering. In his honesty unto death we have the highest expression of the incandescence of the human and the divine in man, the supreme revelation of what it means to be human.

It is in the light of Jesus' unconditional commitment to the kingdom of God that we must define the essence of discipleship under him. Discipleship consists, above all, in total self-dedication to the creation of a new human community, in which love will replace violence, service will replace the brute exercise of power, in which no barrier will separate man from man, in which the first will be the least of today, namely, the wretched and the dispossessed of the earth. Such commitment will necessarily call for preparedness to lay down one's life, wherever those who wield political power act as agents of oppression. The disciple of Jesus is, more than anyone else, a political animal condemned to death; he cannot be greater than his Master.

NOTES

1. Alan Richardson, *The Political Christ* (London: SCM, Philadelphia: Westiminster, 1973), pp. 41–44.

2. Paul Winter, "Sadducees and Pharisees," in *Jesus in His Time,* ed. Han Jürgen Schultz (London: SPCK, and Philadelphia: Fortress, 1971), pp. 47–56.

3. Jeremias, NTT, p. 71

4. Fernando Belo, *Lecture materialiste de l'Evangile de Marc* (Paris: Cerf, 1975), p. 217.

5. *Ibid.,* p. 243 and footnote.

6. *Ibid.,* pp. 287–89.

7. *Ibid.,* pp. 250–55.

VIII

Meeting God
in the Fullness of Man

Every domain of life, whether economic, social, or political, has a depth-dimension, a dimension of transcendence, where the human impinges on the divine, where our proximate concerns merge into the ultimate concern. In the decisions and deeds that go to make up everyday experience, the depth-dimension is only implicitly perceived, as something that inspires us from within or beckons us from beyond, as a presence or an absence. What is thus existentially experienced becomes articulate in the form of symbols, verbal or actional. Thus formulas of faith as well as rites, rubrics, norms, and institutions come into being. It is this articulate expression of the depth-dimension of individual and collective life that we traditionally call religion.

Just as economic, social, and political life can become alienated, so too religion can deteriorate and become untrue to its own essence. As an expression of man's transcendence, religion, more than anything else, ought to stand for his freedom from everything that imprisons him within narrow walls. But where it has ceased to draw nourishment from the original encounter with the Absolute, it loses its meaning and becomes mere dead wood. Instead of helping man to transcend himself and march ahead, it chains him to a dead past or a decaying present.

This is what had befallen Jewish religion in the time of Jesus. It had deviated from its original purity and had even become an obstacle to the realization of the divine purpose in history. The overgrowth of religious beliefs and practices weighed heavily on the common man, crippling what was genuinely human-divine in him. Jesus reacted to the situation in the same manner as did the prophets. He set out to free his people from false religion. This he did by criticizing the religious status quo and by revealing what true religion should mean.

Mercy, Not Sacrifice

Jesus told his contemporaries that cult, divorced from existential encounter with God, has no meaning. And for him encounter with God is possible only when man encounters his neighbour in self-giving love. Human love is the privileged locus where God unveils his presence. Therefore any cult not born of brotherly love is an aberration and an exercise in futility. This is the burden of his saying: "If, when you are bringing your gift to the altar, you suddenly remember your brother has a grievance against you, leave your gift where it is before the altar. First go and make your peace with your brother and only then come back and offer your gift" (Matt. 5:23–24). Peace with man is an essential condition for cult to be meaningful as a symbolic expression of peace with God.

Similarly Jesus rejected those practices of cult which have no impact on life. "Not everyone who calls me 'Lord, Lord' will enter the kingdom of Heaven, but only those who do the will of my heavenly Father" (Matt. 7:21). Not the number of prayers and supplications offered, but effective surrender to the demands of God assures membership in the New Humanity. Proliferation of cultic practices can easily become a substitute for meeting the challenges of life. Jesus therefore advised his disciples to cut out verbosity in prayer: "In your prayer do not go babbling on like the heathen, who imagine that the more they say the more likely they are to be heard. Do not imitate them. Your Father knows what your needs are before you ask him" (Matt. 6:7-8).

Jesus went a step further and proclaimed the primacy of love over cult. This comes out clearly in his conversation with the lawyer as reported by Mark. To the lawyer's question as to which was the greatest commandment of all, Jesus replied: "Love the Lord your God with all your heart, with all your soul, and all your mind, and with all your strength." The lawyer then said to him: "Well said, Master, you are right in saying that God is one and beside him there is no other. And to love him with all your heart . . . and to love your neighbour as yourself—that is far more than any burnt offerings or sacrifices." The Evangelist concludes the story with these words: "When Jesus saw how sensibly he answered, he said to him, 'You are not far from the kingdom of God' " (Mark 12:28-34). To recognize the primacy of love over sacrifices and burnt offerings is in itself to draw near to the kingdom of God. How much more living it out! Jesus used the same principle of the centrality of love to justify his befriending the outcasts of society even at the risk of violating the rules of cultic purity. He told his accusers: "It is not the healthy that need a doctor, but the sick. Go and learn what that text means, 'I require mercy, not sacrifice' " (Matt. 9:10-13).

To understand the full significance of the reversal of values Jesus affected by affirming the primacy of love over cult it is necessary to study his attitude to the Jewish law. For many of the prevailing laws had themselves to do with the practice of cult. Besides, his criticism of law will give us a deeper insight into the nature of the love whose primacy over cult he affirmed.

Man Was Not Made for the Sabbath

Man's existential encounter with God normally translates itself into a system of norms. Thus every religion develops its own complex of laws. The Ten Commandments represent the crystallization into law of the religious experience of the Hebrews. In course of time, around the nucleus of the commandments there sprang up other laws, prescriptions, and taboos, which subsequently found written expression in the first five books of the Bible. The written law underwent further elaboration when, after the exile, the lawyers set out to apply it to the concrete situations of everyday life. Thus an oral tradition was formed which eventually gained normative value comparable to that of the written law itself. According to the scribal calculation the commandments and prohibitions of the written law already numbered no less than 613. With each of them again giving rise to many oral traditions, Judaism had degenerated into a religion of legalism and casuistry. To what ridiculous extent casuistry went can be gauged from the nature of the controversies the lawyers used to indulge in. To cite but two examples, it was hotly discussed whether it was a sin to eat an egg laid on the Sabbath, and whether wearing an artificial tooth amounted to a violation of the law that forbade carrying burdens on the Sabbath. [1]

By falling into legalism of this type Judaism had betrayed its own true essence. The stress was no longer on what man *was* but on what he did or did not do. Besides, since laws, however elaborate, could not cover the whole of individual and social life, the areas left out fell outside the pale of morality, as though they had no depth-dimension and were God-less. Finally, the proliferation of laws made impossible demands on the common people, who could not reconcile strict observance with the requirements of day-to-day life.

Himself a teacher, Jesus had to take a stand in regard to the interpretation of the law. His fundamental attitude comes into bold relief in the following incident: "One Sabbath he was going through the cornfields: and his disciples, as they went, began to pluck ears of corn. The Pharisees said to him, 'Why are they doing what is forbidden on the Sabbath?' He answered, 'Have you never read what David did when he and his men were hungry and had nothing to eat? He went into the House of God, in the year of Abiathar the High Priest, and ate the sacred bread, though no one but a priest is allowed to eat it, and even gave it to his men.' He also said to them, 'The Sabbath was made for the sake of man and not man for the Sabbath' " (Mark 2:23–27). For Jesus the sole purpose of the law was the good of man. The law was but a means, and not an end in itself. Where it prevented the satisfaction of a basic need such as hunger, it ceased to have any binding power. David therefore did the right thing when he defied the accepted taboos regarding the eating of consecrated loaves and shared them with his companions. If so, his disciples, too, did nothing wrong in violating the Sabbath to satisfy their hunger.

It is significant that Jesus does not relate the observance of the Sabbath to the glory and honour of God. The Sabbath was *set apart*—which is what *sacred* means—for divine worship. Therefore one would have expected him to say, "The Sabbath is for the honour of God, who alone is Lord over it." The reason for his failure to do so can only be that in his eyes the honour of God is the fullness of man. It is in man's face that the glory of God shines forth. This tallies also with his identification of man's love for his kind with the love for God. Where man is loved God is loved. Similarly man honoured is God glorified. There is for Jesus no dichotomy between humanism and religion.

If one's own good is sufficient justification for the violation of the Sabbath, how much more the good of others! To those who criticized him for healing a man with a withered arm on a Sabbath day he said: "Is it permitted to do good or to do evil on the Sabbath, to save life or to kill?" (Mark 3:4). The meaning is clear: If the Sabbath is for the good of man, an act of goodness like healing can only be in keeping with the original intention of the law. Any law that forbids doing good to others is by that very fact null and void. More so, if it sanctions evil. Hence Jesus' violent attack on the institution of corban based on the legal provision that if someone had a grudge against his aged parents, he had only to make a fictitious dedication of his wealth to God in order to be freed of any obligation to support them. Referring to this practice Jesus said: "Thus by your tradition, handed down among you, you make the commandment of God null and void" (Mark 7:9–13).

The same protest against the law that kills the spirit may be discerned in his criticism of the prevailing rules of ritual purity, especially those concerning the washing of hands before and after meals. Originally only priests were bound by the rules regarding the washing of hands, and that too only when they ate the tithe or the priestly offering. Subsequently the Pharisees also took over the practice. Possibly they expected the common people to follow suit. Neither Jesus nor his disciples had any scruple in disregarding these rules. When the latter were accused by the Pharisees of eating with defiled hands, he defended them saying: "Isaiah was right when he prophesied about you hypocrites in these words: 'This people pays me lip-service, but their heart is far from me: their worship of me is in vain, for they teach as doctrines the commandments of men.' You neglect the commandment of God to maintain the tradition of men" (Mark 7:6–8). The rules of purity are man-made. And those who hold them up as God-given end up by frustrating the original intention and purpose of God himself. In the beginning God created everything, and found it good. Then came man on the scene, ruling certain things pure, and others impure. What is worse, the very persons who classified things into pure and impure failed to look into the evil that bred in their own hearts, vitiating everything they said or did. In their concern for external cleanliness they neglected the cleanliness of the heart; i.e., sincerity and truthfulness. Thus they fell into inauthentic existence. Jesus therefore invited his critics to turn their gaze from mere externals to the centre of their being and see there the matrix of all evil: "Nothing that goes into a man from outside can defile him; no, it is the things that come out of him that defile a man" (Mark 7:15). It is from the 'heart'—which in biblical usage means the centre of personhood where thinking, feeling, and loving converge and have their common root—that evil proceeds. In other words, it is the fundamental attitude of man that renders things meaningful or meaningless, good or bad, pure or impure. It is man who confers meaning and value on the world around him; not the other way around. Jesus thus affirmed the supreme dignity of man as the creator of meaning and value.

Understood in this sense, Jesus' teaching on ritual purity is a charter of freedom for the human spirit. He declared null and void all irrational taboos based on ignorance and superstition. From now on man can move freely in the world unafraid of being defiled by it. He can approach with inner freedom sex, eating, drinking, love, and friendship. He can without moral inhibitions seek the company of all irrespective of caste, colour, class, or community. The whole world of things, persons, and deeds become capable of mediating truth, beauty, and goodness. The universe is rendered transparent, without unchaste demons inhabiting every nook and corner.

Jesus directed his criticism not only against the oral tradition but also against the written law, which no Jew dared to do until his day. His radical stand on ritual purity is itself a criticism of the rules laid down in Leviticus (11:1–15:33) and Deuteronomy. He radicalized the written law by extending its demands beyond observable actions to the domain of thoughts and desires, to that intimate sphere of existence beyond the pale of social control where man is alone with himself. "You have learned that our forefathers were told, 'Do not commit murder; anyone who commits murder must be brought to judgement.' But what I tell you is this: Anyone who nurses anger against his brother must be brought to judgement" (Matt. 5:21–22). Again, "You have learned that they were told, 'Do not commit adultery'. But what I tell you is this: If a man looks on a woman with a lustful eye, he has already committed adultery with her in his heart" (Matt. 5:27–28). What Jesus envisages here is a new type of man, who in the very depths of his being is responsive to the demands of God, who has no inner recesses where he may take refuge from the God who pursues him.

Jesus went even to the extent of abrogating specific precepts of the written law. He forbad swearing, which the law permitted. "You are not to swear at all . . . Plain 'Yes' or 'No' is all you need to say; anything beyond that comes from the devil" (Matt. 5:33–37; Exod. 20:7). Swearing implies that words uttered in ordinary conversation do not have that claim to truth which statements made under oath have. Jesus, on the contrary, demanded that every word uttered be true and binding solely in virtue of its having been uttered by man. Not anything outside him, but the integrity of his whole life should be the guarantee of truthfulness. Here also the call is to authentic existence, in which one speaks what one *is*. Equally forthright was his rejection of the law of retaliation. "You have learned that they were told, 'Eye for eye, tooth for tooth.' But what I tell you is this: Do not set yourself against the man who wrongs you. If someone slaps you on the right cheek, turn and offer him your left" (Matt. 38–42; Exod. 21:24). Evil cannot be conquered with evil. It should be met not in the weakness of anger but in the strength of love. The tide of evil can be driven back only by releasing the creative energies of love locked in human hearts.

We have already seen how Jesus repealed the Mosaic law of divorce and reaffirmed the indissolubility of marriage (Mark 10:1–11). He likewise repudiated the Old Testament notion of divine vengeance on the enemies of Israel. This may be deduced from the fact that in quoting the Scriptures he leaves out those verses containing the idea of vengeance.[2] Such omissions take on their full meaning when seen against the background of his teaching on the universality of love characteristic of the reign of God. "You have learned that they were told, 'Love your neighbour, hate your enemy.' But what I tell you is this: Love your enemies and pray for your persecutors; only so can you be children of your heavenly Father, who makes his sun rise on good and bad alike, and sends the rain on the honest and the dishonest. . . . There must be no limit to your goodness, as your heavenly Father's goodness knows no bounds" (Matt. 5:43–48). By asking his hearers to love also their enemies, i.e., non-

Israelites, he broke the narrow shell of nationalism within which Judaism had imprisoned itself. Here as elsewhere his vision transcends all bounds and reaches out to the Total Man.

But, did not Jesus sanction the law in its entirety when he said, "Do not suppose that I have come to abolish the Law and the prophets; I did not come to abolish, but to complete" (Matt. 5:17)? The saying means no more than that he considered it his mission to bring the Old Testament revelation to its final completion. This he did precisely by stressing the original purpose of the law, which was the realization of love. He fulfilled the law by transcending it. One may still press the objection by pointing out the subsequent saying in Matthew: "If any man therefore sets aside even the least of the Law's demands, and teaches others to do the same, he will have the lowest place in the kingdom of Heaven, whereas anyone who keeps the Law, and teaches others so, will stand high in the kingdom of Heaven" (Matt. 5:19). It is now generally recognized that the statement as it stands could not have come from Jesus himself, since it is at variance with the fundamental thrust of his teaching and practice. Its origin is to be attributed to the Evangelist himself, who in this context has toned down the radicalism of Jesus to meet the missionary needs of the Palestinian Christian community.[3] The same tendency to domesticate Jesus for reasons of expediency is also to be found elsewhere in the Gospels, as also in the history of the Christian churches.

Woe to the Religious Elite

If Judaism had become a religion that oppressed the spirit of man it was mainly due to the teaching and practice of its religious leaders: the Pharisees, the doctors of the law, and the priests.

The Pharisees considered themselves the true Israel 'set apart' from the common folk. In contrast to the masses, they scrupulously observed the rules regarding the payment of tithes, ritual purity, and the practice of prayer and fasting. But in spite of, or even because of, their strict observance of the law, they were far from God. For they sacrificed the inward to the outward, reality to shadows, the central to the peripheral. Jesus lashed out at this hypocrisy of theirs: "You pay tithes of mint and dill and cummin; but you have overlooked the weightier demands of the Law, justice, mercy, and good faith. . . . Blind guides! You strain off a midge, yet gulp down a camel! . . . You clean the outside of cup and dish, which you have filled inside by robbery and self-indulgence! Blind Pharisee! Clean the inside of the cup first; then the outside will be clean also . . . You are like tombs covered with whitewash; they look well from outside, but inside they are full of dead men's bones and all kinds of filth. So it is with you: outside you look like honest men, but inside you are brim-full of hypocrisy and crime. . . . You snakes, you vipers' brood, how can you escape being condemned to hell?" (Matt. 23:23–33).

In equally incisive language did he criticize the doctors of the law, who were professional theologians officially ordained and invested with the right to act as teachers and judges. They were authorized to make binding decisions in religious and civil matters. But they used their learning and authority to impose insupportable burdens on men and to exploit them in various ways. It was of them that Jesus said: "They make up heavy packs and pile them on men's shoulders, but will not raise a finger to lift the load themselves" (Matt. 23:4). They use religion as a means to maintain and enhance their standing in society. They "like to have places of honour at feasts and the chief seats in synagogues, to be greeted respectfully in the street, and to be addressed as 'rabbi' " (Matt. 23:7). Hypocrites, "they say one thing and do another" (Matt. 23:3). Hence the rebuke: "You shut the door of the kingdom of Heaven in men's faces; you do not enter yourselves, and when others are entering, you stop them" (Matt. 23:13).

Jesus criticized also the official priesthood, the supreme guardian of the religious power structure. However, the target of his attack was not the lower ranks of priests spread all over the country but the priestly aristocracy in Jerusalem. His crucial confrontation with the religious authorities occurred on the occasion of the cleansing of the temple we commented on in an earlier chapter. His charges against them fall under three categories: First, they failed to safeguard the sanctity of the temple by allowing the pilgrims to use its court as a thoroughfare for carrying goods. Second, by misusing 'the court of the gentiles' they violated the latter's right to worship in the temple. Third, by organizing commerce and money exchange in the temple precincts they exploited it to fill their coffers.

This critique of religion is at the same time the inauguration of a new form of religion that has its focal point in man's encounter with the living God who acts in history. In other words, Jesus shifted the axis of religion from the realm of cult and law to that depth-dimension of personal-social life.

The Secular Jesus

Jesus lived what he taught. The centre of his life lay not in cult but in man's history with God.

By Hebrew law he was a layman, not a priest, priesthood being the hereditary right of the members of the tribe of Aaron and Levi. He was born of a tribe "no member of which has ever had anything to do with the altar" (Heb. 7:13). He did not claim to be a priest. Nor was he acclaimed as one by the common folk, by his disciples, or by his opponents. The Gospels do not represent him as one who lived by, for, and around the altar. We do not see him offering sacrifices or organizing public worship. Not the altar but the world was the centre of his life.

It is in the heart of the world that he met his God—at weddings, at festal meals, by the lake-side where fishermen cast and hauled their nets, by wayside wells where the womenfolk came to fetch water, at gatherings of people in the company of outcasts, in the fellowship of his disciples, in the togetherness of friendship, and in the innocence of children. The mustard seed growing into a mighty tree, the yeast leavening a huge mass of dough, the fishes hauled ashore, the fig-tree putting forth its early shoots, the hen gathering her young under the wings, the earth yielding a hundredfold, all these mediated to him the presence of God. It was in and through the myriad facets of the life of his people that he communed with the God of his fathers.

His final meeting with God, his death, was no less a secular event. It was not in the temple of Jerusalem, the centre of Jewish cult, that he met his end. His was not even 'a happy death' assisted by priests chanting supplications for the 'departing soul'. He was killed outside the 'Holy' City on the 'profane' hill of Calvary. He died the utterly secular death of a political criminal. But was not his death at least a sacrifice? Not if by sacrifice we understand the offering of gifts symbolizing man's self-surrender to God. For him death was not a symbol, it was reality itself, the reality of a life lived out in self-giving to God in his fellowmen. If his blood was poured out 'for many', so is the blood of any man poured out in the service of others.

NOTES

1. Rudolf Bultmann, *Primitive Christianity in Its Contemporary Setting,* trans. Reginald Fuller (London and New York: Nelson, 1964), p. 7.

2. For example, in reading from the scroll, "The Spirit of the Lord is upon me . . . " (Isa. 61:1 ff), he omits what follows "the year of the Lord's favour": "a day of vengeance of our God." Compare Isa. 35:4, "See, your God comes with vengeance, with dread retribution he comes to save you," and what follows: "Then shall blind men's eyes be opened, and the ears of the deaf unstopped," and so on, and the message to John the Baptist, "The blind recover their sight" . . . (Matt. 11:2–6). See Jeremias, NTT, pp. 206–07.

3. Jeremias, NTT, p. 211.

IX

Existential Liberation

Up to now we have been critically examining the response of Jesus to the cosmic, social, political and religious bondages of his people. Now it remains for us to see how he reacted to what we termed at the beginning of this book as the bondage within. We shall leave out of consideration the problem of psychic determinisms originating in the subconscious and the unconscious, since it could not have been perceived as such by Jesus or by his contemporaries. In this chapter we shall focus our attention only on three fundamental issues: ignorance about the meaning of life, the ambivalence and vulnerability of freedom, and the experience of life as being-unto-death.

Admittedly, Jesus could not have posed these questions in the same terms in which we frame them. We of the twentieth century have a more articulate awareness of our existence as subjects than people of earlier ages. The conquest of nature through science and technology has sharpened our awareness that we are not mere playthings in the hands of blind cosmic forces but real subjects of history. Besides, the capitalist system in which we live, with its dominant ethos of private interest and competition, tends to reduce each man to an island, thus forcing him to look at the nakedness of his own subjectivity. Finally, researches in psychology have brought to

light the existence of the subconscious and the unconscious in man and their influence on conscious decision
and behaviour. For these reasons the problems of subjectivity have assumed new dimensions of meaning that
they did not have for our forebears.

In the earlier stages of their history the Israelites led a
tribal life. What mattered then was not so much the
individual as the group. The consciousness of the individual was subsumed under that of the collectivity. It
was only later, at the time of the monarchy, that the
individual as such emerged. With that the problem of
individual destiny began increasingly to occupy Hebrew
minds.[1] Still the individual as subject had not completely
come into his own. It is probable that even at the time of
Jesus his emergence was an ongoing process. It is therefore but natural that in his time the problems of subjectivity were not acutely felt or sharply focused. This being
the case, it would be futile to look for a clear formulation
or discussion of them in the Gospels. Such problems
were existentially experienced rather than consciously
and explicitly articulated. Probably, even that existential
experience was only inchoative and germinal when
compared with our own. The following reflections are,
therefore, nothing more than an attempt to draw out
what is implicitly contained in the message of Jesus.

Discovery of Ultimate Meaning

Nowhere in the Synoptic Gospels does Jesus pose the
problem of the meaning of life in abstract, philosophical
terms. In the Bible the notion of meaning, when applied
to human existence, tends to coincide with that of the
good. A person is good if he is as he ought to be. The
entire message of Jesus may be characterized as a call
addressed to man to become what he ought to be, in
other words, to pass from inauthentic to authentic exis-

tence. The call is made not only to individuals but also to the community as a whole. Communal life is meaningful in the measure in which it approximates to what God intended it to be. And what God intends as the final outcome of the historical process is the realization of his reign, the maturation and plenitude of the New Humanity. The communion of all with one another and with God is the horizon of utlimate meaning. That man, individual and community, will meet God, and in meeting him, achieve the fullness of meaning is an essential feature of the message of Jesus. "How blest are those whose hearts are pure; they shall *see* God." It is in seeing the face of God that man will see his own true visage and discover his true identity. It is from God that he will receive his true name. The name each man gives himself is a false name or at least an inadequate one. Truer is the name others give him. Truest of all is the name he receives from God. For God to name is to create. And the name whereby God will call each man will express his true essence as a member of his household: "How blest are the peacemakers; God shall *call* them his sons."

It would, however, be wrong to think that man will meet God apart from, or over the heads of, his fellowmen. It is in the radiance of the myriad human faces that surround him that each man will discover the face of God as well as his own true visage. It is the millions who call him 'brother' that constitute him as a son of God. For God is not outside the human community. He is the depth-dimension of the love that binds the many into the one.

For the individual as well as for the community the final revelation of meaning is a matter of hope. Man is ever a pilgrim in search of him who renders everything meaningful. This does not mean that life is like passing through a tunnel whose end alone brings us to the realm of light. Absolute meaning reveals itself to us, though only inchoatively, in the here and now of everyday life. It is experienced not only as an absence but also as a presence. And there are privileged moments when the Presence is so intense that it grips us at the very roots of our being and radically reorients us from within.

In order to take hold of this Presence or, rather, to be taken hold of by it, man has to remain inwardly open to it. This inward openness is an essential element of the faith that Jesus demanded from his hearers. Meaning remains hidden from all those who shut themselves up within the shell of their own self-sufficiency. That is why Jesus could speak of God's "hiding these things (that is, the things concerning the birth of the New Humanity in the heart of the old) from the learned and the wise, and revealing them to the simple" (Luke 10:21). The same idea seems to underlie the following saying: "To you the secret of the kingdom of God has been given; but to those who are outside everything comes by way of parables, so that (as Scripture says) they may look and look, but see nothing; they may hear and hear, but understand nothing; otherwise they might turn to God and be forgiven" (Mark 4:11–12). Joachim Jeremias has shown that what we have here is a detached saying which has nothing to do with parable proper. The term *parable* here stands for the original Aramaic word, *matla*, meaning 'riddle'. According to him the original would be: "God has disclosed the mystery of his reign to you, but to those outside everything happens in riddles . . . *unless* they return and God forgives them."[2] It is significant that *turning to*—which is what conversion means—is indicated as a prerequisite for understanding the hidden purposes of God. There are truths that can be known only by the pure of heart, by those who are prepared for unconditional surrender and for the risk of total love. Ultimate meaning unveils itself only to those who in faith and love remain open to its presence.

To encounter meaning is to arrive at a moment of decision. And where the ultimate meaning is in question, the decision has to be radical, affecting life in its entirety. It requires putting on a new mind and a new heart. The call of absolute meaning assumes priority over all other concerns and requires the relativization of all other values. "The kingdom of Heaven is like treasure lying buried in a field. The man who found it, buried it again; and for sheer joy went and sold everything he had, and bought that field" (Matt. 13:44–46). More, he who has encountered the ultimate meaning and has made a radical option in favour of it has to remain faithful to it, cost what it may. "No one who sets his hand to the plough and then keeps looking back is fit for the kingdom of God" (Luke 9:62).

The decision required by encounter with meaning has to be translated into practice—personal and social. The meaning perceived has to be endowed with a body; it must find structural expression in the customs, laws, and institutions of society. The aim of practice is to bring individual and society closer to their own ultimate horizon of meaning. To do so is to create new meanings. And to create new meanings is to encounter the ultimate meaning at a deeper level. The appropriation of meaning is a spiral movement from the encounter to praxis and from praxis to deeper and richer modes of encounter, and so on indefinitely. It is on purpose that we qualify the process as indefinite, for neither encounter nor praxis will exhaust the possibilities of ultimate meaning. Even with the realization of the New Humanity, the Absolute will remain not only a presence but also an absence.

Jesus not only taught but also embodied in his own

person in a unique manner the meaning of life. His teaching was not something added on to his life. It was the radiance of his life itself. To encounter him is to be in the presence of someone whose word and deed somehow reveal the meaning of *all* human existence. In his openness to the Absolute, in his unconditional loyalty to the reign of God, in his resolute opposition to evil in every form, in his single-mindedness, in his stubborn refusal to compromise, in his undaunted courage in facing the consequences of his commitment, in his encompassing sympathy for the poor and the outcast—in all this we have a concrete manifestation of what it means to lead an authentic life.

Reintegration of Freedom

Man is the only being on earth that is always more than what it actually is. Every other being has set limits, definite boundaries. They change and grow within certain foreordained limits. Man, on the contrary, is always reaching out beyond himself into the infinite. He lives and moves within an absolute horizon that confronts him with unconditional demands. At every step he is faced with an 'ought'. He cannot ignore this 'ought' without denying himself. The 'ought' implies that he has the capacity to act in accordance with it. In fact freedom consists precisely in the spontaneity with which man grows into what he ought to be. It consists less in the possibility of choosing between good and evil than in the self-unfolding of the spirit unto the good and the true.

But freedom as the spontaneous doing of what one ought to do, as the joyous pursuit of the good and the true, is more an ideal to be striven after than a quality man already possesses. If in actual life he often does what he ought to do, it is not without struggle and suffering. The pursuit of the good is accompanied with tension, conflict, anxiety, and doubt. He is often torn between the urge to do good and the temptation to do evil, as though in the innermost recess of his soul there is a rupture and a division. In consequence he is a prey to internal instability and insecurity. He finds himself vulnerable at the centre of his selfhood. He faces the constant threat of falling away from the pursuit of the good. He realizes that he is condemned to the frightening possibility of using his freedom to hate rather than to love, to inflict death rather than to bestow life, to demolish rather than to build up. In short, freedom itself appears to him as a burden and a bondage. It is this crucial problem that St. Paul had in mind when he wrote: "I discover this principle, then: that when I want to do the right, only the wrong is within my reach. In my inmost self I delight in the law of God, but I perceive that there is in my bodily members a different law, fighting against the law that my reason approves and making me a prisoner under the law that is in my members, the law of sin. Miserable creature that I am, who is there to rescue me out of this body doomed to death?" (Rom. 7:21–24).

The ambivalence and vulnerability of freedom is at the root of sin; i.e., one's failure to do what one knows one ought to do. Repeated sins react on the character of the individual and predispose him to deviate further from the good. In this way freedom becomes all the more vulnerable. Moreover, sins leave in the doer a sense of guilt, which paralyses his spirit and cramps his creativity. It is to this complex of vulnerability, sin, and guilt that we refer when we use the term 'bondage of sin' in this chapter.

The bondage of sin is to a considerable extent historically and culturally conditioned. In any society the rigorous enforcing of obsolete and inane laws and the proliferation of ever-new ones create a sense of spiritual impotence among the people. In consequence, such laws are honoured more in their breach than in their observance. Those who violate them in bad faith become burdened with the sense of guilt. Similarly, economic exploitation and inhuman social conditions force the poor to take to thieving, prostitution, and the like to make a living. Thus structural sin begets personal sins. Conversely, the personal sinfulness of individuals may give birth to structural evils in society in the form of dehumanizing laws, institutions, and customs.

How did Jesus respond to the challenge of liberation from the bondage of sin? His radical criticism of law and cult strikes at the social roots of sin. His teaching on man's being the master of the Sabbath means that the violation of laws does not constitute a sin where these do not serve the good of man. The same conclusion may be drawn from his criticism of cult. The primacy of mercy over cult that he proclaimed removes the very source of much useless guilt feeling among believers who fail to observe all the minute observances prescribed by traditional religion. Furthermore, he abolishes every form of obligation in the sense of 'being bound', insofar as he makes love the fundamental principle of all human striving. And where there is love there is no sense of being bound. Or, rather, love is both necessity and freedom in one. To be bound by love is the supreme realization of freedom.

However, Jesus was concerned less with the social basis of the bondage of sin than with its roots in the heart of man. And the roots of man can be healed only if he is open to the forgiving love of God. This, in a nutshell, was his answer to the problem of human frailty, sin, and guilt. To grasp its meaning fully it might help to reflect on a human analogy.

It is a matter of common experience that love is a force

that heals and integrates man. He who is not loved feels inwardly insecure and vulnerable when faced with the innumerable demands that the world makes on him. He lacks that vital milieu in which alone he can be truly spontaneous and free. But the day he receives genuine love from man or woman, he undergoes a profound internal change. He finds his moorings, feels secure and rooted in the centre of his being, in the centre of *all* being. The wide range of possibilities and options, which used to confuse and bewilder him, become from now onward subordinated to his new-found love. His life takes on direction and meaning. What is more, before the person he loves he regains spontaneity. The experience of love dissolves all that inhibits and constricts him. Even his failures and defects cease to be a burden to him. He knows that he is accepted as he is with all his shortcomings. In short, the invasion of love from without brings about a reintegration of his personality and frees him from his internal shackles. All this is true in its own way also of a person's relation to society. The love of the community shown through recognition, acceptance, and forgiveness heals and reintegrates its members from within. This is the basis of our hope that a truly socialist society in which the person is recognized as the supreme value will have a therapeutic effect on its members and will help release their creative energies.

Now, if the limited, and in itself ambivalent, love of our fellowmen can help heal and reintegrate us from within, how much more can divine love!

Jesus brought the good news that the forgiving love of God is always there for man to take hold of. Divine forgiveness is available to all those, only to those, who are poor, i.e., those who recognize their need for it. The first beatitude must be understood in the exclusive sense to mean: "Only the poor have the blessings of God." In fact Mark says so explicitly: "I came to invite not virtuous people, but sinners" (Mark 2:17). Similarly, the saying: "I tell you this: Tax-gatherers and prostitutes are entering the kingdom of God ahead of you", means: "Publicans and prostitutes will enter the kingdom of God, and not you."[3] The supreme generosity of divine forgiveness comes into bold relief in the parable of the prodigal son. The father of the family does not wait for the son to come and fall at his feet asking for pardon. On the contrary, while the son "was still a long way off his father saw him, and his heart went out to him. He ran to meet him, flung his arms around him, and kissed him" (Luke 15:20).

Jesus describes the forgiveness of God as a creative, saving force that touches man in the depth of his being, where he is alone with himself, and refashions him from within. He expresses this idea in the language of symbols. Forgiveness is compared to the remission of debt where the debtor is freed from bondage to the money-lender (Matt. 18:27). It is likened to bringing home a lamb that had strayed away and got entangled in a mesh of briars and thorns (Luke 15:5). Here too the idea of liberation is stressed along with that of the offer of security. The son who erred is welcomed back, clothed in the best robes, offered ring and shoes—all of which are gestures whereby the father recognizes him as a free man. Forgiveness brings about also the reconciliation of the sinner with the community. The prodigal son is received back into the family to enjoy once again the freedom that belongs to him as a son. From now on he is like one risen from the dead.

The power of forgiveness to remould man from within is brought out still more clearly in the story of the adulterous woman who wetted Jesus' feet with her tears, wiped them with her hair, and anointed them with myrrh. To the Pharisee, his host, who was scandalized at this, Jesus said: "I tell you, her great love proves that her many sins have been forgiven; where little has been forgiven, little love is shown" (Luke 7:47). It is not said that her sins were forgiven, *because* she loved much. Just the opposite is what is meant: She loved much because she was forgiven much. In other words, it was the experience of divine forgiveness that made her capable of loving much. That experience touched the core of her being and released the powers of loving that were atrophied. If love is what is most human in man, then we may say that forgiveness humanized her. Love is also that act which is supremely free. If so, we may equally say that forgiveness, by activating her capacity to love, brought her inner freedom. It saved her from internal disequilibrium and vulnerability. Elsewhere in the miracle stories, the recreative effects of divine forgiveness are represented as overflowing into the body and rendering it whole.

What is remarkable about the teaching of Jesus is that he views divine forgiveness as something that man can mediate to his fellowmen. It was the gracious presence and words of Jesus, the man from Nazareth, that communicated the forgiving love of God to the woman of ill fame. Similarly, when he told the paralytic, "Your sins are forgiven", he was not claiming to be the ultimate source of forgiveness. (The use of the passive is a device the Hebrews resorted to lest they profane the name of God.) What he meant to convey was: "God has forgiven you your sins." Jesus was not more than the vehicle that conveyed to the sick man the forgiveness of God. In fact any man may become the instrument of divine forgiveness, as is clear from the prayer Jesus taught his disciples, "Forgive us the wrong we have done, as we have forgiven those who have wronged us" (Matt. 6:12). What we have here is not a petition that God may forgive

us *in the same manner as* we forgive others or *because* we
forgive others, but a declaration of our willingness to
pass on to others the forgiveness we ourselves have
received. The petition may therefore be paraphrased
thus: "Grant your forgiveness to us who are ready to
mediate it to our fellowmen." Where man forgives his
neighbour we have a revelation of the forgiveness of
God. It is in the measure in which he experiences the
liberating forgiveness of God that he becomes capable of
liberating others from internal insecurity, sin, and guilt.

However, man is not a mere passive recipient of divine
mercy. The reverse of divine forgiveness is repentance
on the part of man. The offer of forgiveness is accompanied by the call to repent. Repentance demands the
restructuring of one's whole life, a coming back to one's
senses (Luke 15:17), a recognition of one's guilt, and a
preparedness to be reconciled to others and give up
one's evil ways (Luke 19:8–9; Matt. 5:23–24; Mark
10:17–31). If repentance and divine forgiveness produce
identical effects, does not the one render the other
superfluous? The problem resolves itself when we
realize that the relation between the two is dialogical. It is
divine forgiveness that disposes man to repentance.
Conversely, it is repentance that makes him inwardly
attuned to receive the forgiveness of God, which heals
and restructures him at his roots.

Love Is Stronger than Death

What is the use of winning freedom from ignorance
and sin, if such freedom as is won is doomed to succumb
to the necessity of death? It is small consolation to sug-
gest that mankind as such will continue to exist even if
individuals die and disappear from the scene. Are individuals mere tools that some blind destiny makes use of
to achieve its inscrutable ends only to discard them once

they have served their purpose? Are they mere stepping-stones to help humanity climb higher and higher until it reaches the New Heaven and the New Earth? Let us see what light the message of Jesus sheds on the problem of individual survival.

It is necessary to see things in historical perspective. The early Hebrews did not believe in any real survival after death. They saw the dead confined to a desolate region called Sheol and endowed with some sort of shadowy existence. It is only in the postexilic writings that we find traces of belief in an afterlife and resurrection, which, in all probability, the Jews took over from the Persians or the Egyptians. In the time of Jesus it was the Pharisees who believed in resurrection. The Sadducees, on the contrary, rejected such a belief as alien to the original revelation contained in the Pentateuch.

It is beyond doubt that Jesus shared the Pharisaic belief in the resurrection of the dead. In order to discredit belief in resurrection the Sadducees posed him the following question: If the dead rise from the dead, whose wife will a woman be in the life to come, who while on earth was wife to seven brothers consecutively, all of whom died without leaving any children? Jesus replied: "You are mistaken, and surely this is the reason: you do not know either the scriptures or the power of God. When they rise from the dead, men and women do not marry; they are like angels in heaven. But about the resurrection of the dead have you never read in the Book of Moses, in the story of the burning bush, how God spoke to him and said, 'I am the God of Abraham, the God of Isaac, and the God of Jacob'? God is not God of the dead but of the living" (Mark 12:18–26). If God declares himself as being in the present the God of the patriarchs, the latter could not have just succumbed to death forever. The argument of Jesus may not be convincing, but his mind is clear enough. Elsewhere in his reply to the disciples of John the Baptist he includes the resurrection of the dead in the blessings of the New Age: "Go and tell John what you have seen and heard: how the blind recover their sight; the lame walk, the lepers are made clean, the deaf hear, *the dead are raised to life,* the poor are hearing the good news" (Luke 7:22–23).

Belief in some form of survival after death is presupposed also in the teaching of Jesus on righteousness and its reward. Man's conduct here and now is of decisive significance for his absolute future. "Be careful not to make a show of your religion before men; if you do, no reward awaits you in your Father's house in heaven. . . . Do not store up for yourselves treasure on earth, where it grows rusty and moth-eaten, and thieves break in to steal it. Store up treasure in heaven, where there is no moth and no rust to spoil it, no thieves to break in and steal" (Matt. 6:1, 19–20). Note that the reward promised will be realized not in the present alienated existence but 'in heaven', in other words, in the New Humanity.

What is it that entitles man to membership in the New Humanity that is not subject to death? Here we meet with an astounding paradox in the teaching of Jesus, namely, that he promises reward only to those who do not seek any reward. "But you must love your enemies and do good; and lend without expecting any return; and you will have a rich reward" (Luke 6:35). Not self-interest but self-giving is what asssures survival after death. Those who live for their own selfish ends will forfeit the true life. "Whoever seeks to save his life will lose it; and whoever loses it will save it, and live" (Luke 17:32–33). Now, to give without expecting a return is the essence of love. If so, there is a strict correlation between love and the true life that does not succumb to death.

Underlying his teaching is a conception of history as made up of two opposing currents—one leading to decay and death; the other, to life that endures forever. The current of life is in the final analysis God as self-giving love, living and working in history. He is at work giving himself to men and gathering them into a community of love. Man has the frightful option to identify himself either with the current of death or with that of life. He opts for death when he makes his fragile self the centre of all and reduces his fellowmen to a position of means to his ends. This, in the language of Jesus, is what is meant by 'seeking to save one's life'. Those, on the contrary, who, like God, give themselves to others in service insert themselves in the current of life that carries them forward into the absolute future that lies beyond death. Belief in the resurrection expresses the hope that God accepts the live of those who surrender themselves to him by living for their fellowmen. Therefore it is also a challenge addressed to man to affirm the forces of life, such as love, friendship, cooperation, and the solidarity of all, and to fight the forces of death—illness, poverty, egoism, hatred, injustice, inequality, and oppression. Only those will rise to new life who help their fellowmen break the fetters that chain them to powers that kill both body and soul.

At this point a word of caution is in order. Survival after death as taught by Jesus is not to be confused with the immortality of the soul. This latter concept was smuggled into Christianity from Greek philosophy. In contrast to the Greeks, the Hebrews did not conceive of man as a soul imprisoned in a body. For them man was a unity, an animated body rather than an enfleshed spirit. The soul was nothing but the inwardness of the body, and the body nothing but the outwardness of the soul.[5] They could not, therefore, have conceived the existence of the soul without the body. In their eyes any survival was bound to have a bodily dimension. It is along the same lines that Jesus, too, must have conceived the destiny of many after death. It is equally probable that he could not have thought of the resurrection of the individual apart from the community of men. For Hebrew thinking, the body, not the soul, was the principle of human solidarity.[6] The body was also the basis of continuity with the material universe. Presuming that Jesus shared the Hebrew mode of thinking, we may conclude that he too thought of individual survival as intimately bound up with that of the community and of the material world. But how are we to concretely envisage individual survival after death? To this question Jesus does not give any answer. Possibly he did not know the answer. Or he would answer as he did the Sadducees: You do not know the power of God.

NOTES

1. Gerhard von Rad, *The Message of the Prophets*, trans. D.M. Stalker (London: SCM, 1968; New York: Harper, 1972), p. 200.

2. Jeremias, NTT, p. 120.

3. *Ibid.*, pp. 116–17.

4. *Ibid.*, p. 201.

5. John A.T. Robinson, *The Body: A Study in Pauline Theology* (London: SCM, 1966), p. 14.

6. *Ibid.*, p. 15.

X

Jesus and the
Oppressed of Today

In the life and message of Jesus we witness the emergence of a new force in history for the liberation of man, a force at once human and divine, subversive and constructive. For those who have encountered him he represents the most powerful and authentic expression hitherto of man's striving for fullness of being. He is a brother to all who believe in the brotherhood of man, a friend to all who look forward to the dawn of the age of freedom. As a quester after freedom he can be a source of light and inspiration to the millions in India who are groaning under the weight of organized oppression. In this concluding chapter we shall try to show how his message can become a creative force for the liberation of the Indian masses. We shall deal only marginally with the problem of existential liberation, not because it is unimportant but because it has all along received sufficient attention, whereas liberation from the social system and the system of values has been sadly neglected.

The question regarding the relevance of Jesus for social liberation today could be raised from two different standpoints. First, from the standpoint of one who is not a disciple of Jesus but has a certain appreciation of his person and message, and is open to the conviction that he may have something relevant to say. Thus a Hindu, a Muslim, or even a Marxist may study the Gospels and derive from them inspiration and guidance for radical commitment. Second, from the standpoint of a disciple who has encountered Jesus and identified himself with his faith, commitment, and destiny. A disciple is personally involved with his master and, therefore, cannot view his teaching in a spirit of detached objectivity. It is in the spirit of personal loyalty that we are approaching the problem.

The Jesus–Community

No disciple of Jesus is an island. He is related to other disciples in time and space. The roots of his discipleship go back to the past, to the simple Galilean fishermen whom Jesus called that they may *be with him*, i.e., share his vision and commitment, and to the millions of others who have laid down their lives for his cause. He is also in communion with his counterparts all over the world. He is thus inserted into an invisible fellowship of men and women, one in their oneness with Jesus. Let us call this fellowship the Jesus-community. It is in solidarity with this Community that we are raising the problem regarding the relevance of Jesus for human liberation. The answer too depends, to a great extent, on the self-understanding of the same Community. For it is primarily through this fellowship of his disciples that the Jesus of yesterday can become present to the oppressed of today. A few reflections, therefore, on the nature of the Community may be found useful.

What distinguishes the Jesus-community from all other religious communities is its being centred upon Jesus through sharing his faith and hope. Now, the object of Jesus' faith and hope was the God ahead who is to come to sum up everything. Every fibre of his being, all the energies of his soul and body are strained to that ultimate future. Hence to be centred upon him means for the disciples to be drawn into a current that carries them beyond him to God. Their destiny as disciples is to march with him to the unknown ahead. They are essentially a community of pilgrims.

But the God of Jesus is one who is at work in the world fashioning the New Humanity by giving himself to all, irrespective of caste, creed, community, race, region, or culture. Of this universal community the fellowship of disciples is only a fragment. Hence the paradox: What distinguishes the Jesus-community is its belief in the New Humanity, which does not admit of any distinction. A disciple of Jesus has, therefore, to accept as brothers all those to whom God reveals himself in whatever way he chooses. He must further recognize that those outside the Community may have encountered God at a deeper level than those within. If so, the Community is not a sect opposed to other sects; nor does it represent a religion opposed to other religions.

All this represents a departure from past Christian attitudes. There was a time when Christians believed that those who did not share their faith were barred from the road to salvation, and therefore went all-out to convert them. Eventually, when the theology of conversion became discredited, they began to think of their mission in terms of developing the underdeveloped, an approach based on the, to them, comforting assumption that they themselves were developed while others were not. In recent times, the concept of development having gone out of vogue, they have started chanting the slogan of liberating the unliberated. All through these developments one thing remained constant, namely the conviction that they were the 'haves' and the rest the 'have-nots'. The Community has to disown this arrogant, self-righteous understanding of their mission in history. They must recognize, and rejoice in, the fact that those outside are being saved, developed, and liberated to the degree to which they respond to the challenge of God in history. Their mission consists not so much in work *for* the liberation of others as in seeking liberation *with* others. They have as much to learn from others as others have to learn from them. The only thing they have and others do not, is their personal encounter with Jesus as mediating the presence of God. It follows from this that their presence and action in the world has always to be ecumenical in the sense of being-with-all and working-with-all.

For the Community, to be centred upon Jesus is to follow the way he showed. He did not seek to establish the reign of God by means of economic, social, and political power. He refused to turn stones into bread, just as he shunned the path of political messianism. His attitude to secular power is particularly relevant today, living as we do in a society that is becoming progressively secularized. Secularization means the vindication of society by reason of its own relative autonomy vis-à-vis faith and organized religion and, as such, points to the coming-of-age of man. It must be welcomed as an instance of the self-liberation of man in history. The Community therefore has no right to claim any special competence in secular matters in virtue of its religious faith. Nor is it empowered by its faith to exercise any secular authority over fellow citizens. As regards, for instance, the organization of production or the structuring of political power, it has no exclusive source of knowledge. In these matters it has to depend as much on reason as any other group of citizens. By recognizing this it will have a clearer understanding of the limits within which it has to work for the construction of a better world, and therefore also of the need for dialogue and collaboration with others.

These preliminary reflections on the nature of the Community must be understood as applicable to all that we are going to say on its liberating role in India. One more word of caution: The reader should not conclude from our discussion thus far that commitment to liberation is something added on to the nature of the Community viewed as already constituted in itself. The Community *is what it does*. It has to fashion its nature in the very process of commitment. It is therefore less an institution than a 'project' in the root sense of the word. It is always in the process of becoming what it is, what it ought to be.

Keeping Hope Alive

The mission of the Jesus-community is the same as that of Jesus, namely, to set the oppressed free. In order to fulfil this mission it must first of all quicken and sustain man's hope in the New Humanity as the ultimate point of arrival of all struggle for liberation.

Hope is not just one virtue among others, like chastity or patience, which one may fail to practice and yet live. It is the very climate of the human spirit, the air it breathes in order to live. To lose hope is to die, is to lapse into nonbeing. This holds true of the individual as well as of society. When, for instance, someone takes up a profession, he is making an act of hope that he will be able to cope with the task. When a boy and a girl decide to marry, they do so in the hope that they will be true to each other and be able to meet the demands of life together. Similarly, when a people opt for a new model of society they do so in the hope that they will be able to create and maintain it. All those who undertake teaching the young, or reforming the deviant, harbour the hope that their efforts will bear fruit in the future. Where hope has withered away, individuals end their lives, families disintegrate, political systems collapse, and the educational system comes to a standstill. If so, hope is a constituent of all secular life, whether individual or collective. Of this secular hope, religious hope is the depth-dimension. The latter comes to the foreground when, for example, the professional, the politician, or the educationist is willing to sacrifice everything else for the sake of his or her respective hope. What renders everything else relative can only belong to the dimension of the absolute.

If hope is the mainspring of history, any crisis affecting it bodes ill for the future of man. There are in fact symptoms of such a crisis in India: the widespread cynicism of the intellectuals, the deep sense of frustration found among the exploited masses, their servile, almost fatalistic submission to exploitation, the loss of idealism among the youth, and the dearth of committed leadership at all levels. The underlying vacuum of hope has to be filled if India is to march forward to a more just and humane society.

Who will fill this vacuum? Hinduism has still to exploit the wealth of its tradition in order to develop a vision of history fully in harmony with the self-understanding of contemporary man. Marxism, with its hope in a classless society, did in fact fill the vacuum up to a point, especially in the early stages of its presence in India. Unfortunately, it has in the meantime come to terms with the power politics of a caste and class society. As a result the concept of classless society itself is fast degenerating into a sort of opium for the masses. Christians too have sinned against their hope by substituting for the New Heaven and the New Earth either the salvation of souls or the power and prestige of their respective churches.

Hence the relevance, more than ever, of Jesus' hope in the New Humanity as the absolute future of man. The oppressed masses will find in that hope a powerful motivation for radical action. Besides, by living within the horizon of their absolute future they will feel inwardly free from the tyranny of the past with its obsolete laws, institutions, and customs, and from an uncritical clinging to the present. It will foster that detachment which is so necessary for permanent revolution. Where it is lacking the revolutionaries of today will end up as the conservatives of tomorrow.

Hope in the New Humanity should not be regarded as alien to the people of India. It is implicit in the very longing of the oppressed masses for better days ahead. Even their hopelessness today presupposes that hope. Nor does the Jesuan hope stand in irreconcilable opposition to the original Marxian vision of the classless society, the latter being but a secular version of the former. The very dialectical thinking that helped Marx project the goal of a classless society also underlies the thought and language of Jesus, if not of the entire Bible. For what is the reign of God but the negation (the final supersession) of the negation of man (consisting of illness, death, inequality, domination, and sin)? In saying this we are not overlooking the basic difference that for Jesus the negation of negation is the work of man in dialogue with God, whereas for Marx it is to be achieved solely through collective human effort. But do not Marxists affirm in the act of uncond:tional commitment what they deny in theory? The scope of this chapter forbids our enlarging upon this theme. Suffice it to remember that the hope in the New Humanity is in accord with the implicit aspiration of the masses and with the fundamental thrust of the

Marxian vision. It is this convergence of hopes that provides the basis for common effort for the liberation of the masses.

The ultimate hope is not a product of creative phantasy but a life-force sustaining individual and collective life. Therefore it cannot be instilled in the masses solely through writing, preaching, or propaganda. Of course, art, literature, and the mass media can to some extent be used to instil that hope. But the more powerful generators of hope are to be sought at the level of social practice. What is the use of trying to communicate hope in a classless society to a people who have little hope of earning enough bread for the morrow or of breaking loose from the clutches of the moneylender? Hope grows only where chains are broken, barriers overcome, and walls pulled down.It dies out where man is not able to overthrow the oppressive structures of the present. There is, therefore, no more effective way for the Community to create and foster collective hope in the New Humanity than to participate in the day-to-day struggles of the people. Such participation is necessary also to legitimize and validate its own hope. For how can it proclaim the New Humanity as the fulfilment of history if it chooses to live outside the main current of history? How can it bear witness to the New Age as the fruit of theandric dialogue if it refuses to have dialogue with the God manifesting himself in the life of the people? How can it hold up the Total Man as the final goal of liberation if it shuns holding hands with the fragments of humanity around?

But is not the Jesuan vision of the New Humanity incapable of inspiring the man of today, considering that it is conceived as the end of history, and therefore also as the end of all creativity, quest, friendship, and love? True, traditional Christianity has popularized the notion of 'the end of the world'. The term is wrong if taken in the literal sense; right if taken in the dialectical sense. The New Age is not the end of history in the sense in which we speak of the end of colonialism in India. What ends history cannot, at the same time, fulfil it. The New Age is therefore the end only of history as we know it, of the history of man's alienation. In a very true sense it is equally the dawn of the authentic history of man, of a history, still, of quest, growth, friendship, love, and creativity.

Towards a Penultimate Model

The ultimate horizon of hope will always remain an asymptotic concept, i.e., one that can never adequately express the reality it signifies. It belongs to the order of legitimate myth. In fact the perception of the depth-dimension of any reality can be expressed, if at all, only in symbols and myths. The mythical character of the ultimate hope is at once a strength and a weakness: a strength because only myths symbolizing the ineffable can elicit commitment unto death. They alone can galvanize men into concerted action, appealing, as they do, to the conscious as well as the subconscious, to the rational as well as the emotional. None will lay down his life for an abstract system of philosophy or for a dry economic formula. That is why every revolution hitherto has projected its own array of myths. The mythical character of the ultimate hope is also a weakness and a limitation. For the mythical cannot provide concrete guidelines for action here and now. To become an operative concept it has to crystallize into a workable project, which is what we mean by the penultimate model.

The manner in which this model has to be formulated can be none other than the manner in which the ultimate hope itself emerges in human consciousness. The latter, we have seen, is not just an empty dream or phantasy. It takes shape in consciousness through a spontaneous negation of the evils of today. In formulating the penultimate model we are but making explicit the path of negation taken by the human spirit in projecting the ultimate hope. Negation here is to be understood dialectically as implying also an affirmation of whatever is true and good in the existing conditions. In addition, it has to be based on a scientific analysis of the prevailing social system and its ideology.

Any model, however scientifically constructed, will necessarily be provisional. It will need constant revision in the light of subsequent experience. The model thus revised will become the basis for further action, which in turn will demand a further revision of the model, thus indefinitely. Though provisional at any given stage, it may call for unconditional commitment until it once again proves itself to be inadequate.

The construction of such a model is, understandably, an ecumenical and interdisciplinary task. The Community alone is not competent to formulate it. It can, however, bring the Jesuan vision of man and his destiny to bear upon the desired model so that it is in harmony with the integral good of man. To give but one example, it cannot derive from the message of Jesus any concrete programme for the reorganization of the bureaucracy. It can, however, demand that the bureaucracy be so structured as to promote the responsibility and the initiative of all citizens, and criticize any model that is not likely to fulfil this condition. With these formal considerations in mind let us now approach the problem of determining the content of a new model of society for the people of India. Prescribing a detailed model being out of the question, we shall confine ourselves to indicating the main structural principles that should guide its formulation, principles derived from our introductory analysis of Indian society.

CONTINUITY WITH THE PAST

Centuries of foreign domination and colonialism have made us materially and mentally slaves. Our economy is still, to a considerable extent, geared to the benefit of foreign capitalism or Soviet socialism. We are likewise subjected to a steady and powerful cultural invasion from the West to which we all too easily succumb. Even the refuse of Western civilization finds an honoured place on our altars. We are progressively being reduced to a nation of cultural bastards. The colonial menality has taken such deep root in the country that we can envision our future only in terms of imported models, whether American, Soviet, or Chinese. Now the time has come to reverse this trend by rediscovering our own soul and establishing continuity with the past. This is not a defence of chauvinism or a plea for revivalism, but an appeal to construct a model incorporating the genuine values of our tradition. For only a society with deep roots in the past can promote true creativity.

PRODUCTION FOR THE PEOPLE

As regards the national economy, the existing disparities in wealth and income can be abolished only through need-based production and equitable distribution. By need-based production we mean a system of production that gives priority to meeting the essential needs of the masses rather than to promoting conspicuous consumption on the part of the rich. Equitable distribution means apportioning income according to the service one renders to society (not according to discriminatory norms such as the superiority of intellectual over manual work)

and, insofar as resources permit, also according to the
objective needs of people, so that those who, for no fault
of their own, are unable to contribute their share of
work—children, the sick, the cripples, the aged, and the
unemployed—will have enough to have a decent life.

SOCIALIZATION

It would, however, be wrong to think of human wel-
fare solely in terms of production and consumption. As
long as people have no control over the economy, a
society with a high degree of consumption can be more
dehumanizing than another that is able to provide only
the bare necessities of life. Hence the need to stress the
principle of socialization. Socialization does not consist
in the equal distribution of the means of production,
which, even if feasible, would mean not the abolition but
the universalization of private property with its ethos of
private interest and competition. Neither is it to be
equated with nationalization which, instead of abolish-
ing wage labour, reduces every citizen to the position of
an employee of the state. True socialization demands
that society as a whole at the various levels of its organization determines the ownership and the use of the
productive forces. In a fully socialized society there will
no longer be private property understood as the absolute
right to use and to misuse. All property will be either
personal or communitarian: the former being owned by
individuals but used in accordance with the will of the
community as a whole; the latter being property owned
and used by the community, whether it be of the village,
the panchayat, the district, or the state.

SOLIDARITY

In a truly socialist society there cannot be any
dichotomy between economy and politics, between the

community of producers and the community of citizens. In such a society political decisions will also be a productive force; and the producers, active participants in political decisions. With this reservation in mind, let us consider the main principles that should determine the political structure.

One such principle is that of solidarity. The political community must be organized in such a way that the free development of all will be the condition for the free development of each. No individual or group should be allowed to use society as a whole as a means for furthering their own ends. No one should be able to march ahead to a higher level of economic well-being or of culture without at the same time carrying along with him his weaker brothers. This means striking at the very roots of laissez-faire and individualism. However, the solidarity aimed at should not be that of feudal society based on personal loyalty and dependence or of caste and joint-family, whose members were not real centres of decision. Nor should it be equated with that of dictatorship, which reduces the citizens to the level of mere things. What we should strive to achieve is a solidarity of persons as centres of decision and creators of their own destiny. Our aim should be a form of human togetherness deriving from each one's concern and responsibility for all. Hence our initial formulation of the principle of solidarity must be read also in the reverse order to mean a society in which the free development of each will be the condition for the free development of all.

SUBSIDIARITY AND PLURALISM

In order to promote the free development of each we should, in constructing a model, adhere to the principle of subsidiarity. Subsidiarity requires that what any lower unit of society can accomplish should not normally be undertaken by a higher unit. For instance, what is within the competence of the individual should not be taken over by the family or the village community. Similarly, what the latter can do should not be done by the district or the state. Subsidiarity, therefore, implies the decentralization of power and decision making. The function of the state in the new order of things must not be to rule by dictates from above but to promote and coordinate initiatives from below, i.e., from the community of persons.

If subsidiarity is necessary to prevent over-centralization and dictatorship, respect for pluralism is necessary to prevent solidarity through rigid uniformity. India is a vast country with many religions, races, and regional cultures, each having its own distinctive genius. Socialism does not require the levelling down of all these differences. It is not barrack communism. The different cultures and subcultures must be allowed to grow and bear fruit. Similarly the uniqueness of each individual as a source of creativity must be cherished and fostered. So too, associations and fraternities representing diverse talents and interest must be encouraged so long as they do not hamper the common good.

A penultimate model in accord with the principles we have enunciated demands a new type of man, with a new consciousness, vision, and sense of values. What should the content of that new consciousness be? What should be the nature of law, morality, philosophy, and religion in the new society? What should be their function vis-à-vis economic and political life? These and similar questions, though crucial, cannot be gone into here. One thing, however, needs to be said: In the new social order there should be no place for class consciousness based on class exploitation. Nor should there be any law, morality, philosophy, or religion emanating from the privileged classes and calculated to safeguard their interests. All forms of consciousness will have to draw nourishment from society as a whole and reflect its struggles and hopes.

Prophetic Protest

From our discussion so far one might be tempted to draw the conclusion that the Jesus-community is concerned more with the future than with the present, especially if one is used to thinking of the future and the present in terms of either-or. The future, whether proximate or ultimate, is not to be seen as a rival to the present. We have seen that it is in the present that the ultimate hope is encountered. It is equally the consideration of the present that enables us to construct a model for the future. In either case we are thrown back on the present. The present was also the central concern of Jesus. In fact what distinguished him from the prophets that went before was his message that the reign of God was already germinating in the present. It was he who for the first time invited his contemporaries to turn away from the excessive preoccupation with the future or the past and listen to the call of the present, of the present that summed up the past and was pregnant with the future. He demands the same attitude from his Community today.

READING THE SIGNS OF THE TIMES

If the New Humanity is silently growing in our present history it is important for us to learn to recognize its presence. For how else could we take a stand in relation to it? That is why Jesus enjoined on his listeners to read the signs of the times. The signs are not just any event or situation but only those that carry significance for the ultimate future of man. In order to discern them one has to ask whether the event or situation in question contributes to the fullness of man or not. Seen in this light, whatever embodies or fosters freedom, love, equality, cooperation, and solidarity are positive signs of the times; whatever does not, negative signs. In many cases such discernment is easy enough; in others, truth is far different from what appears on the surface. For instance, putting up exclusive hostels for the benefit of Harijan boys and girls may seem a positive step in the direction of helping the underprivileged. But a little reflection is enough to show that such hostels will only perpetuate caste inequality. Where social process or political movements are concerned, it is necessary to supplement or even correct mere impressionistic evaluations with social analysis.

The type of social analysis required for the correct reading of the signs of the times must fulfil certain conditions. It must, first of all, be structural, i.e., aimed at unveiling the dehumanizing character of the social system as a whole, not merely its superficial inadequacies. It is not enough, for example, to ascertain the depth and extent of poverty in India. What is needed is to lay bare its structural causes and show how they are detrimental to the true development of man. Analysis must also be global, covering not only the laws and institutions of society but also the domain of ideology and human subjectivity. Thirdly, it must be futurological, by which we mean that it should bring out the long-term consequences for man of the social facts under study. Finally, it must be scientific, as regards not only the tools of analysis but also the data it makes use of. The Community must take into consideration the result of analysis conducted along these lines before making sociopolitical options. In other words, it must combine the prophetic and the scientific in one single commitment.

FOSTERING THE ENERGIES OF THE NEW AGE

The Community reads the signs of the times in order to act upon them. And its action will have to be twofold: fostering the energies of the New Age to come (the positive signs of the times) and fighting the forces of dehumanization (the negative signs). Its role in society is to be a two-edged sword that cuts to heal as well as to destroy. Its mission resembles that of the prophet Jeremiah, who was sent by Yahweh "to pull down and to uproot, to destroy and to demolish, to build and to plant" (Jer. 1:10).

The positive social trends in India that need nurturing are many: the substitution of feudal loyalty with loyalty to goal-oriented associations and political parties: the organization of the working class; the politicization of the masses; the process of secularization; the progressive interdependence, in practice and consciousness, of the different castes, classes, races, and regions; the erosion of feudal ideas and values; the spread of a genuinely critical attitude to religion; the revolt of the youth against bourgeois morality; the transition from elitist to people's literature and art. These trends are, admittedly, riddled with ambiguity and internal weaknesses. Still they are to be welcomed as representing the gropings of the people of India towards the horizon of the New Humanity.

Of all the humanizing forces the most significant are the socio-political movements of protest against prevailing conditions. The political parties inspired by the teachings of Marx and his followers have been in the vanguard of the people's struggle against feudal and capitalist forms of exploitation. They have to their credit the organization of the urban and rural proletariat in many parts of India. Very recently the Sarvodaya, which believes in a sythesis of Marxism and Gandhism, has come forward as the champion of the oppressed, especially in Bihar. Even in the more conservative Congress there are critical individuals and groups sincerely committed to the eradication of social injustice and inequality. Finally there is the wordless protest written large on the faces of the exploited millions whose collective resentment can, given the right kind of leadership, break out into open revolt.

NOT PEACE BUT THE SWORD

The disciples of Jesus cannot but make their own every form of legitimate protest in the country. They should in fact feel a certain spontaneous affinity with all who denounce the oppression of man by man, since they cherish the memory of Jesus, who had to pay the price of death for his option to protest. To refuse to join in the protest against injustice is to disown the God of the poor whom he proclaimed and join the ranks of his enemies, who make a living by killing the souls and bodies of men; it is a form of practical atheism.

Unfortunately the socio-political movements of protest in India suffer from many limitations. They are often based on an inadequate or even false analysis of society and, therefore, are incapable of delivering the goods. Their leaders are also victims of dogmatism and ideological fixation. There is not enough self-criticism and independent thinking among them. Besides, the forces of protest neutralize one another, for their leaders indulge in mutual hatred and suspicion. For these reasons the Community cannot fully identify itself with any of the existing radical movements. Neither can it ignore them; for despite their present limitations they alone have a record of service to the people. Such being the case, the most it can do is to offer them critical collaboration on issues where there is sufficient consensus. Meanwhile it must also strive to provide a common platform where radicals of differing convictions can meet and sort out their differences.

However, neither critical collaboration nor efforts to reconcile warring radical factions seem to be adequate to meet today's challenge. The existing leftist movements resemble ancient decaying trees that are no longer capable of putting forth fresh shoots. There is little hope that they can be rejuvenated either through critical collaboration from without or through participation from within. Therefore, the most urgent need today is the creation of a new socio-political movement of liberation with a clearer perception of goals, a more adequate methodology of action, a truly committed leadership, and with a broader base among the masses. The cynicism of the common man in the more politically conscious States of India regarding all existing political parties is clear proof that the time is ripe for such a venture. Nothing less than a new movement for liberation can mobilize the revolutionary potential contained in the silent protest of the masses.

The Community has to protest not only against the existing social system but also against the failure of its own leaders to protest when protest was their bounden duty. What protest the latter made till recently was highly selective in regard to its target. They fumed with moral indignation when their minority rights were tampered with; but showed little concern when the rights of the underprivileged, who form the majority, were brutally violated. They protested vehemently against those who called in question the traditional sexual morality; but callously closed their eyes to the inhumanity of a social system that forces thousands of innocent girls to take to prostitution in order to make a living. They roared in anger against those who defended the legitimacy of artificial contraception; but chose to be silent in the face of an economy that condemned millions of children to illness and premature death. In their zeal for the unborn they forgot about those others who had the misfortune to be born. True, in recent times they have come out with radical pronouncements on social justice. But, that these were not seriously meant became abundantly clear when they disowned and victimized the few who tried to put the teaching of their leaders into practice.

Freedom through Revolution

Protest must be translated into action for the radical restructuring of society and the fundamental revision of its ideology. The transformation aimed at must also be rapid. Resigning ourselves to a gradual transition to a more just society will amount to condemning generations of men, women, and children to subhuman existence. The rapidity of change is, up to a point, conditional upon certain objective factors, such as the extent of corporate production, the progress of mass media, and the degree of organization of the masses. But much more decisive are the subjective factors related to the conscious intervention and free decision of men. The objective need for change must also become a subjective, felt need. The intensity with which the members of a society experience the contradiction between the prevailing system and their own emergent self-understanding will largely determine the speed of change. And when a people commit themselves to bringing about radical and rapid change through conscious and planned intervention they are opting for social revolution as distinguished from social evolution.

But revolution should not be understood merely in the narrow sense of overthrowing the social system. Its goal is, in the final analysis, the creation of a new man; and, since what distinguishes man from animals and the world of things is consciousness, it is, at the same time, the creation of a new consciousness, consisting in a new sensitiveness, a new sense of values, and a new vision of the world. A merely structural revolution will prove itself self-defeating where there has not been a corresponding revolution of consciousness. For new structures, however perfect, are liable to be exploited by individuals and groups to serve their own selfish ends.

If the goal of revolution is the creation not only of a new social system but also of a new consciousness, it is evident that the process of revolution itself must be such as to give birth to that consciousness. In other words, there must be a continuity between the consciousness of the future and the consciousness of the men of today who create the future. How could a people ruled by private interest and lust for power usher in a society in which each person will see in the good of all his own good? How can those moved by envy, hatred, and revengefulness create an order in which man's greatest need will be his fellowmen? How can selfishness beget concern for others, hatred beget love, competition beget cooperation? Hence the need to stress the importance of developing the right type of revolutionary consciousness.

If revolutionary consciousness is itself a process of growing into the consciousness of the new man it is clear that it cannot be viewed merely as a means for overthrowing structures. What is the very source of human creativity cannot be made subservient to any of its own functions or creations. Man is greater than the structures he brings into existence. The growth of revolutionary consciousness is therefore not only a step towards structural revolution but also a realization, however partial, of revolution itself. The radicals who forget this are likely to fall victim to discouragement and frustration when they see the goal of structural revolution receding into a distant future. If as a result of their action some more people have become critical of the status quo and concerned about the fate of their weaker brothers and sisters, they can rest assured that they have already sown the seeds of total revolution.

What should be the content of revolutionary consciousness? In answer we can provide here only a few general observations. The consciousness in question must, first of all, be critical; i.e., it must include an awareness not only of the fact but also of the extent and the mechanisms of exploitation and dehumanization. Secondly, it must be practical, in the sense of being oriented to—and, wherever possible, born of—concrete involvement in the struggle for liberation. Thirdly, it must be humane, i.e., instinct with gentleness, kindness and an encompassing concern and compassion for all. Fourthly, it must be communitarian, by which we mean that the consciousness of the many must fuse into one collective subversive force, which, naturally, is not possible without organization of the exploited. Fifthly, it must be prospective, having for its goal the construction of a new model of society. Finally, it must have the character of the unconditional and the ultimate, lest revolutionists, having put their hands to the plough, look back or, what is worse, betray the cause of revolution for lesser values.

Revolutionary consciousness and revolutionary practice are dialectically interrelated. They condition and draw nourishment from each other. No revolutionary action is initiated without there being people conscious of the evils of the status quo and of the need for a new social order. The quality of action, too, depends on the quality of consciousness. The reverse is also true. It is through actual involvement in subversive action that the revolutionary elite and the masses gain a deeper understanding of the structures of exploitation and of the type of society they want to construct. However, it is not enough to regard the relation between consciousness and practice merely as one of mutual conditioning. For it might create the false impression that active participation in struggle is an essential prerequisite for *any*, even provisional, revolutionary consciousness. It is closely bound up with freedom from existential bondage. Religious teachers, educators, doctors, psychiatrists, and social workers have evolved their own methods to help individuals solve the problem of psychic determinisms, meaninglessness, sin, and death. Their methods continue to be relevant so long as efforts are made at the same time to create the social conditions necessary for an adequate solution of the problem.

In our discussion thus far we have laid more stress on revolutionary consciousness than on revolutionary practice for two important reasons: First, the creation of revolutionary consciousness does not get the attention it deserves in radical circles today. The stress is unduly on revolutionary practice, and there is not enough criticism of the type of consciousness that inspires it. We have already noted elsewhere the fact of Communists fighting capitalism in the name of the values of capitalism. The second important reason has to do with the mission of the Jesus-community itself. The Community is not a political party though it has a stake in the political life of the people. Essentially a prophetic movement, its primary concern is the self-transcendence of man into the New Humanity which, though realized through economic and political programmes, can never be identified with any of them. And what enables man to transcend himself in response to God, who calls him from beyond, is his consciousness—his vision, faith, and hope. As already pointed out, it is in virtue of his consciousness that he disengages himself, though only in a provisional manner, from the present and projects himself into the future even before he is actively involved either in pulling down the present or constructing the future. If even a provisional revolutionary conciousness is an authentic form of man's self-transcendence in dialogue with God, how much more so is mature revolutionary consciousness. That is why the Community should lay particular stress on consciousness as *the* potential for revolution. This does not imply that it should devalue praxis. It should devalue only uncritical praxis, which hampers rather than promotes the growth of the New Humanity.

Love or Violence?

By virtue of the faith and hope it shares with Jesus, the Community is in conscience bound to work for the liberation of the downtrodden masses of India through a total revolution. But does not revolution necessarily involve the use of violence, which goes counter to the teachings of Jesus?

Violence may be understood in two different senses. It may mean the use of force to effect the mutilation and destruction of persons. It is exercised directly when, for instance, the police or the army kill people; indirectly by those who maintain a system that denies the people the basic necessities of life and thereby condemns them to illness and death. Violence may also be understood in the sense of organized resistance meant to paralyse an existing institution or the social system as a whole. Here the object of violence is not personal but structural. This distinction is important because persons are absolute values, while structures are not. Besides, the two forms of violence need not necessarily imply each other. Structures can be overthrown without harming persons; persons can be destroyed while leaving structures intact. In what follows we use the term violence in the first of the two senses, namely, as force employed to mutilate or destroy persons.

Let us begin with things as they are. The existing social system is itself institutionalized violence against the underprivileged. The guardians of the status quo, the ruling classes, are using the army and the police to employ violence against their opponents either by killing or imprisoning them. How can this huge machinery of violence be met except through violence? If the liquidation of the defenders of the establishment is necessary for the overthrowing of the establishment itself, is it not for that very reason also legitimate?

But, is personal violence really necessary to overthrow the prevailing social system? If the oppressed classes in India have attained the right level of revolutionary consciousness and have been organized into a well-knit subversive force, they can, in our view, effect a radical and rapid social change through collective resistance in the form of strikes, demonstrations, noncooperation, and civil disobedience. Violence is, therefore, superfluous. Nor does it recommend itself as an effective weapon for revolution. Of course, a minority of well-trained militants may succeed in demolishing the present system by resorting to bloodshed, even before the objective and subjective conditions for revolution have ripened. But to maintain the new regime they will have to use violence against their opponents as well as against the

masses in order to make them fall in line with their
demands. Thus revolution will only mark the beginning
of another era of violence. Besides, when the oppressed
resort to violence are they not thereby justifying the
violence of the oppressors? The latter could be as much
convinced of the justice of the prevailing system as the
former are of its injustice. Finally, violence is usually
coupled with the irrational forces of hatred and revengefulness. And, as we noted earlier, an ethos of revolutionary hatred cannot create a truly socialist consciousness. Violence as a weapon for revolution is therefore not
only superfluous and ineffective but also counter-
productive.

Seen from this angle the teaching of Jesus on nonviolence is today as valid as ever. Evil can be overcome not
by countering it with evil but by releasing the powers of
love dormant in the hearts of men. What we need today
is not the organization of violence or the mobilization of
collective hatred but the dissemination of love and concern for others, of a love and concern extending even to
the oppressors. For the oppressors too are in their own
way alienated. None of them can be held individually
responsible for the system of oppression, which, once
set in motion, has a relative autonomy of its own. Besides, the oppressors, by the very fact of their being
such, are themselves truncated men, alienated from
their true social essence. Finally, they are as much subject to existential bondage as the oppressed themselves.
Hence they too are, at least objectively, in need of liberation. All this shows that only a revolution inspired by
universal love, which does not exclude from its concern
even one's enemies, can lead the people to authentic
freedom. The Community, therefore, must consider it
integral to its mission in history to uphold the universal

love Jesus taught as the greatest potential for the liberation of man.

There are, however, historical limit-situations in which love for the defenseless many may legitimize violence against an agressive few, on condition that it is employed in the last resort, and there is a prudent hope of success. But even in that situation it must be a violence of love that excludes all love of violence, all hatred and spite. In any case, in the prevailing conditions, the question is only of academic interest. For we have still to go a long way before we will have conscientized and organized the masses along the right lines, and fully exploited the revolutionary potential of nonviolent, collective resistance.

To sum up, in order to make Jesus' message of liberation relevant for the exploited masses in India, the Community must mobilize all its resources to quicken and nurture collective hope in the absolute future of human-divine fullness, decipher the footprints of God in history, foster the humanizing forces in society, fearlessly protest against everything that makes man less a man, create the right kind of revolutionary conciousness in the masses, help organize collective resistance against structures of unfreedom, and finally, uphold love as the motive, matrix, and end-result of revolution.

However, the disciples of Jesus will be able to fulfil their mission only if they break away from much of the theory and practice of traditional Christianity in India—from its policy of institutional domination, its alliance, covert or overt, with the ruling classes, its subservience to foreign money and foreign centres of power, its feudal power-structure, its legalism and cultism, its hypocritical combining of verbal radicalism with practical conservatism, its spirituality of resignation, its ethics of stoic prudence, and its servile acceptance of imported theologies and ideologies. All this shows that they are today placed in a situation similar to that of Jesus, who had to liberate himself from tradition-bound Judaism in order to be radically honest to God and his kingdom. For them too, as for Jesus, the price of radical honesty will be death. But then, it is necessary for some to lay down their lives that others "may have life, and may have it in all its fullness" (John 10:10).

Bibliography

Bornkamm, Gunther. *Jesus of Nazareth*. London: Hodder and Stoughton, 1960.

Brown, Raymond E. and others (ed.). *The Jerome Biblical Commentary*. Theological Publications in India, Bangalore, 1972.

Bultmann, Rudolf, *Primitive Christianity in Its Contemporary Setting*. London: Fontana, 1964.

———. *Jesus and the Word*. New York: Scribner's, 1958.

Caird, C.B. *Saint Luke*. London: Penguin, 1971.

Cullman, Oscar. *The Christology of the New Testament*. London S. C. M.,1971.

———. *Jesus and the Revolutionaries*. New York: Harper and Row, 1970.

Derret, J. Duncan. *Jesus's Audience*. London: Darton, Longman and Todd, 1973.

Dodd, C.H. *The Founder of Christianity*. London: Collins, 1971.

Fuller, Reginald H. *The Mission and Achievement of Jesus*. London: S. C. M., 1967.

Furnish, Victor Paul. *The Love Commandment in the New Testament*. London: S. C. M., 1973.

———. *Interpreting the Miracles*. London: S. C. M., 1971.

Hunter, A. M. *The Work and the Words of Jesus*. Madras: Christian Literature Society, 1969.

Jermias, Joachim. *Jerusalem in the Time of Jesus*. London: S. C. M., 1969.

———. *New Testament Theology*. New York: Scribner's, 1971.

———. *The Parables of Jesus*. London: S. C. M., 1963.

Kummel, W.G. *Promise and Fulfilment*. London: S. C. M., 1961.

Manson, T.W. *The Sayings of Jesus*. London: S. C. M., 1971.

———. *Ethics and the Gospel. London:* S. C. M., 1966.

McKenzie, John L. *Dictionary of the Bible*. London: Geoffrey Chapman, 1966.

Nineham, D.E. *Saint Mark*. London: Penguin, 1973.

Perrin, Norman. *Rediscovering the Teaching of Jesus*. London: S. C. M., 1967.

Richardson, Allan, *The Political Christ*. London: S. C. M., 1973.

Schultz, Hans Jürgen. (ed). *Jesus in His Time*. London: S.P.C.K., 1971.

Taylor, Vincent. *The Gospel According to Mark*. London: Macmillan, 1966.

von Rad, Gerhard. *The Message of the Prophets*. London: S. C. M., 1969.

(On the Indian situation see notes to Chapter 2)